THE WEISER INDIANS

The Weiser Indians
Shoshoni Peacemakers

by
Hank Corless

Foreword by
Merle W. Wells

University of Utah Press
Salt Lake City
1990

∞ The paper in this book meets the standards for permanence and durability established by the Committee on Production Guidelines for Book Longevity of the Council on Library Resources

Library of Congress Cataloging-in-Publication Data

Corless, Hank, 1945–
The Weiser Indians : Shoshoni peacemakers / by Hank Corless ; foreword by Merle W. Wells.
p. cm.
Includes bibliographical references.
ISBN 0-87480-347-0 (alk. paper)
1. Shoshoni Indians—History—19th century. 2. Shoshoni Indians—Cultural assimilation. 3. Weiser Region (Idaho)—History—19th century. I. Title.
E99.S4C67 1990
979.6'25—dc20

89-40599
CIP

Frontispiece courtesy of Idaho State Historical Society, neg. no. 63-211.18, Jane Gay, photographer.

FOR DWIGHT. MY FRIEND.

CONTENTS

ILLUSTRATIONS

MAPS

"I shall never forget the first and only Indian I ever saw in that country. It was in Indian Valley and Indians were still the subject of scare stories fresh from the lips of those who lived in that time. Like one born out of time, one lone buck, squat and plump, rode through the village. He was riding a round-bellied, scrubby white pony. His saddle was littered with many items of questionable use. He was leading three or four scrawny crowbaits packed with queer trappings. He rode slowly not turning his face once to the curious crowd of youngsters gaping at him from the roadside.

"I have since wondered what was in the mind behind that sphinx-like face shrouded in mystery. His ancestor's fine old hunting grounds were ruined by the whites. Fences clogged the wild birds prairie land; farm houses, black smoke curling from their chimneys kept the game away. Then here were the encroacher's children staring at him, wide-eyed and resentful."

—Mickey Aitken,
Saga of Salubria

FOREWORD

Eagle Eye and his Weiser Shoshoni associates had an extraordinary experience accommodating their traditional way of life to changes imposed by the nineteenth-century ranchers and farmers who settled in their ancestral domain. More than an ordinarily adaptable group, they had Mountain Shoshoni origins that helped them resist pressure to move to a distant Indian reservation in an unfamiliar area. All of Idaho's Mountain Shoshoni people went to a great deal of effort to retain their long-established range. Their ancestors had a tradition of hunting mountain sheep in a wilderness that few other people could penetrate.

Many of them preserved their customs and continued to occupy their mountain strongholds in Wyoming, as well as in Idaho, for two decades after mining and ranching commenced in more accessible areas. Others had shifted to adjacent ranges—notably in Idaho's Lemhi and Weiser valleys—after they obtained horses a century prior to gold rush intrusions into their borderlands. More than other Shoshoni peoples, they succeeded in avoiding removal to reservations. That way, Eagle Eye's Weiser group made a surprisingly successful transition to a new way of life without leaving their old homeland. Other Northern Shoshoni people who inhabited reservations after 1867 had a much less satisfactory time. An important lesson in Indian acculturation can be learned from Eagle Eye's successful program of adaptation to life in a hostile mining and ranching environment.

Unlike Wyoming's Mountain Shoshoni, Idaho's sheep hunters had a long era of close contact with the plateau culture of their Nez Perce neighbors. Occupying a zone of cultural interchange between Great Basin and plateau elements over a long prehistoric period, Idaho's Northern Shoshoni gained additional cultural exposure when many of them began to travel on horseback and to have more contact with Great Plains Shoshoni who expanded from Texas to Saskatchewan and Alberta before 1780. Some Mountain Shoshoni adopted more of a Plains way of life and added long buffalo hunts to their migratory pattern. These included a Lemhi Valley group that ranged into Montana. In addition, a Weiser group farther west occupied a smaller Idaho area.

Shortly after 1800, Idaho's Lemhi and Weiser Shoshoni had an opportunity to add features of a fourth—and very different—cultural variety to their ever-changing way of life. Fur hunters based in Montreal and Saint Louis came to the area with guns, traps, iron utensils, and new economic pursuits. These affected Plains Shoshoni more than their mountain neighbors. Eagle Eye's Weiser people avoided much of that impact for a while, and traditional mountain sheep hunters were hardly disturbed at all. But after 1860, when miners and ranchers suddenly rushed into some of their lands, Eagle Eye and his Weiser Shoshoni had to meet serious new challenges.

Mining pressures affected Eagle Eye's Nez Perce neighbors a year of two before his own people were displaced. Eagle-from-the-Light and his important lower Salmon Nez Perce band (a village led by White Bird after Eagle-from-the-Light retired to Montana in 1875) resisted mining expansion into their territory. But after his call for war against miners in Florence failed to drive all gold hunters from their Salmon River mines, Eagle-from-the-Light moved to join Eagle Eye's Weiser Shoshoni. By 1862, a Boise Basin gold rush brought a worse threat to all Shoshoni of that area. Farm settlements around the lower Boise forced them to move their traditional summer salmon fishing festival north to Eagle Eye's upper Weiser country, where it continued to attract a variety of tribes for another decade and more. Military raids against Idaho's Indians also proved troublesome after 1862. Most army efforts during the Snake War, for instance, focused on finding Shoshoni to fight; but, generally, Northern Paiute and Northern Shoshoni vanished when miners or military showed up. In fact, from early fur trade days, the Shoshoni were noted for their skill in evading intruders who annoyed or threatened them.

Eagle Eye could not avoid central Oregon's Snake War that affected Idaho from 1866 to 1868, and a decade later, his Weiser

Shoshoni experienced more conflict during General O. O. Howard's campaign against Buffalo Horn's Bannock forces. Eagle Eye's sons took great pride in their father's diplomatic skill in avoiding excessive embroilment in that unavoidable disturbance. More importantly, in 1878, Eagle Eye was reportedly killed during the Bannock conflict. That false report helped him considerably during his later career, because hostile army authorities ceased to look for him, and he was able to disappear with his Weiser survivors into Idaho's mountain wilderness. Gradually, he and his extended family underwent a remarkable cultural change that few other Northern Shoshoni could match.

Eagle Eye's consistent and determined refusal to accept reservation life enabled him and his people to acculturate more successfully than most other Northern Shoshoni who could not avoid that alternative. Even though reservations were supposed to promote acculturation, those who lived on them generally failed to do as well as Eagle Eye's group, who stayed on their own land. Eagle Eye and his followers were resourceful enough to go into a mining and lumber business with settlers in Eagle Eye's Dry Buck Basin refuge near the ancient Timber Butte obsidian tool center. A few Nez Perce refugees joined them in an isolated, nonreservation community that lasted until a little after 1900. Eagle Eye, who survived there until 1896, emerged as a highly respected Shoshoni leader who succeeded, largely because he got so little publicity. His descendants—well educated and capable of operating in a new culture as well as in their traditional ways—finally moved to Fort Hall and became reservation leaders.

Many Northern Shoshoni gained prominence through their success in developing large mounted bands that impressed early trappers and settlers by their size and power. Other Northern Shoshoni, particularly Mountain Shoshoni, chose a less spectacular way of life. Eagle Eye's people represent those who followed this more conservative approach, and who finally adapted more successfully because they avoided reservation life and retained their ancient homeland with a tenacity characteristic of their Mountain Shoshoni heritage. Their variety of cultural experiences gave them an importance that most of their neighbors could not duplicate.

Several important aspects of nineteenth-century Indian adjustment to disruption of their traditional culture became evident in a comparison of Eagle Eye's experience with misadventures of other bands exposed to reservation life. More than a few settlers preferred to engage in military campaigns in order to wipe out Idaho's Shoshoni peoples altogether. Such attempts succeeded at Bear River and Salmon Falls, as well as in part of Oregon's Malheur country where an expedition of Idaho miners inflicted substantial damage to Northern Paiute inhabitants. Most Northern Shoshoni managed to elude that kind of military pursuit. With notable exceptions, the majority of Northern Shoshoni survivors were confined to the reservation at Fort Hall where they were expected to become farmers and adopt a new culture. For a decade, they were forced by the absence of resources and by the failure of Fort Hall reservation officials to provide supplies to go in numbers to Eagle Eye's Weiser country each summer. Reservation authorities compiled a poor record in their attempts to force an alien culture upon their Shoshoni and Bannock residents. In retrospect, the Indians' failure can be explained by a natural resistance to agents trying to destroy their traditions and to suppress their culture. Other aspects of unacceptable reservation administration have been identified as well. In contrast to reservation life, Eagle Eye's people preserved their language and organization while they worked in gold mines or sawmills operated by local settlers. Living on their own land, they decided what they wanted to do without having to give up their old ways. Andy Johnson, for example, retained his marvelous ability to tell Shoshoni folk tales while he served as a ditch rider for some lower Boise farmers, men who did not undermine his cultural values. In their transition from hunting, fishing, and camas or bitterroot harvesting to a close association with local settlers in their homeland, the Weisers made lasting friendships and gained protection often denied to reservation bands. Eagle Eye's identity at Dry Buck, for example, was concealed for most of two decades during his later career in that area. His success in overcoming a long period of hostility from miners and ranchers came partly from his good fortune in finding people who would accept him after more than a decade of conflict. Eagle Eye's adaptation to life in a changing world brought together a select group of people who managed to develop an unusual alternative to reservation life for unfortunate Indians. Their arrangement would have been difficult to manage for large Shoshoni bands during that era, but they demonstrated the advantages of a less rigid solution to Indian problems of survival in a region dominated by hostile settlers.

Documentation of Eagle Eye's remarkable career comes from a variety of sources. Sven Liljeblad's ethnographic investigation has provided information essential for interpreting archival and newspaper materials. A careful geographical examination of Eagle Eye's country also has been crucial. In 1962, Eagle Eye's granddaughter—Josephine Thorpe—returned with her family to revisit her childhood home in Eagle Eye's camp. Sixty-six years had passed since Eagle Eye's time, and I acted as guide with Dr. Liljeblad for that expedition. Sites were located, including a major Pacific Northwest obsidian source for prehistoric tools that had remained unknown to archeologists. This find contributed greatly to a clarification of Eagle Eye's story, and has allowed a superior interpretation of Eagle Eye's adventures and cultural importance.

Merle W. Wells

PREFACE

The story of the Weiser Indians is one of both tragedy and triumph. It is the story of the last, free, nonreservation Indians who lived in the valleys of what is now southwestern Idaho, set against the rugged backdrop of the frontier. My first encounter with the history of the Weisers began twelve years ago while I was pursuing a research project. I came across information on these people of the past, and soon found that a detailed study of these fascinating Indians had never been done. I started to collect what little information was available, but it has only been recently that enough material has surfaced to allow the story of the Weisers to be told.

Sources that are available to researchers and historians about other native groups do not exist for these Northern Shoshoni people. There were no missionaries to document the events and life-styles of the Weisers, as there were for the Indians in the northern and eastern part of the state, and the Weisers had no Indian agent assigned to them to make detailed reports on their activities. Still, I discovered a surprising amount of information about them in military reports, territorial government files, and reports of agents from the Office of Indian Affairs. Newspaper files dating since 1867 contain a limited amount of credible knowledge. The most important information in any of these files is several interviews with an original member of the band. In addition to military reports and government files, I have used some secondary sources to clarify certain points, but I have kept their use to a minimum. All my sources are noted in the text, and I alone accept the responsibility for any errors or interpretation of them.

I encountered much difficulty in presenting the Weiser story using, with the single exception, white sources. The early material examined was often inaccurate, biased, or exaggerated, and it was necessary to document by continuously cross-referencing through many historical sources. Further, to verify controversial findings, I drew upon the expert opinions of the most noted scholars in the fields of history, archeology, linguistics, and anthropology, as well as consulting historical and scientific studies and journals.

Writing a history of the Weisers, a band of northern Mountain Shoshoni, involved a close examination of the cultural patterns belonging to the different groups of native people who interacted with them. During the 1860s, southwestern Idaho was inhabited, basically, by two other bands besides the Weisers: a Snake River band of Paiute led by Chief Egan (a Shoshoni himself) and a southern Nez Perce band under the leadership of Eagle-from-the-Light, an important chief known to be hostile to the advancing whites. Thus, the Paiute, the Nez Perce—and other itinerant bands of Shoshoni—interacted with and had far-reaching effects on the Weisers' culture and economy. Recent literature often makes reference to the Weisers as a "mixed" or Paiute band (perhaps because of this confluence of cultures), but my own research makes it clear that they are of Shoshoni origin.

An unclouded written record of the Weiser Indians as an organized group begins in 1867, when they first came to the attention of the white public. Under the leadership of their noted headman, Eagle Eye, the Weiser and Council valleys became the center of an Indian trade network after the Boise Valley was lost to white encroachment. During the years following 1867, the Weisers thwarted government attempts to remove them from their homeland, and managed to keep peace between the white settlers—with whom they willingly shared their country—and the Indian groups who came for the annual rendezvous.

As the tragic events of the 1870s led to open hostilities, however, the peaceful Weisers were caught up in the conflict of the Nez Perce War of 1877 and were forced to seek refuge on the Malheur Reservation in Oregon. Fleeing across the wild regions of Oregon and Idaho during the Bannock War of 1878, the band splintered. Some were killed or taken captive and sent to reservations, while others scattered to isolated areas in the mountains to make a last stand during the Sheepeater Campaign in 1879. Reports and sightings of survivors in the early 1880s ranged from the Seven Devils Mountains in the west, to Loon

Creek and beyond in the east. The Weisers had become phantoms of the forest and seemingly lost to history.

The object of this study is to recreate the story of the Weisers and add a small chapter of literature to the history of the Indian people in what is now Idaho. I offer this attempt in the hope it will be of interest to the general reader and of meaning to the Shoshoni nation.

The process of researching and completing this work involved the aid of a number of distinguished scholars. I am especially indebted to Dr. Merle W. Wells of the Idaho State Historical Society, and Dr. Sven Liljeblad, anthropologist and linguist with the University of Nevada-Reno. Both Dr. Wells and Dr. Liljeblad read the manuscript, offered suggestions for improvement, and contributed from their extensive knowledge on the Weiser people. Many thanks are due to Professor Max G. Pavesic, head of the Anthropology Department at Boise State University, and Patricia K. Ourada, professor of Indian studies there, for their kind assistance and interviews. Professor Jon P. Daley, Department of English, Boise State University, rendered specific help by making his research available. To the staff of the Idaho Historical Library and Archives and the faculty of Boise State University I owe a special debt of gratitude for help in locating rare publications. State Archeologist Tom Green contributed valuable assistance and encouragement toward the completion of this work. My appreciation to Brigham D. Madsen, author and historian at the University of Utah, for the use of his works on the Shoshoni people, for reading the manuscript, and for encouragement. Much is owed to my colleague and friend, Lenard Malmin, who listened patiently to my many recitals and proofread the entire work, and to Ona Siporin who edited the manuscript for publication. Last, I acknowledge my wife, Pam, for the constant support she has provided in this endeavor.

Hank Corless
Boise, Idaho

ONE

Indians in the Weiser Valley

CULTURAL ASPECTS IN HISTORIC TIMES

When Abraham Rinearson rode his horse into the canyon of the North Fork of the Payette River in southwestern Idaho one spring day in 1892, he might have been thinking of any number of things he would find there. He followed the twisting, steep trail above the riverbank, protecting his surveying equipment as he picked his way to Dry Buck Creek. He probably questioned why anyone would want to homestead this part of the country when there were other lands, not as isolated and just as suitable, still available. Except for this trail, he knew, the closest good road was the Round Valley-Smith's Ferry route that led to Squaw Creek. His surprise must have turned to wonder at what he found in that remote canyon of the North Fork.

Tucked away in the wilderness were sturdy log homes next to neat, cultivated gardens. Fruit trees grew near green pastures; cattle and horses grazed on the hillside above a wheat field in the quiet solitude—a quiet broken only by the soothing roar of distant rapids and the sigh of the wind on stands of ponderosa pine and quaking aspen.

Rinearson's astonishment must have been complete, for here, unknown to most of the surrounding white community, was a group of Indians living in the last stronghold of their old homeland. These Indians were remnants of the Weiser band, a small but significant group of Northern Shoshoni who, under the leadership of Eagle Eye, resisted reservation life to the end and yet were, ironically, a major force in preserving peace between Indians and whites.

The purpose of this book is to disclose the story of the Weisers, a band of northern Mountain Shoshoni called Sheepeaters, with Nez Perce and Bannock mixture. Their homeland was the isolated valleys of the Weiser and Payette rivers in west-central Idaho near the Oregon border. In order to unmask their story, it is first necessary to look at what is known about the geography and historic cultures of what is now eastern Oregon, southeastern Washington, Idaho, northern Nevada, and extreme western Wyoming.

In 1867, at the time of white contact with the Weisers, in what we call central Idaho today, there were two major Indian groups: the Nez Perce toward the north and into Hells Canyon, and the Shoshoni located south of the main Salmon River. On the Snake River plains there was a large Bannock population, and in the present-day panhandle region were located small tribes, a group of Kutenai in the northern area being the most significant among them.[1] The Kalispel tribe was north of Lake Pend Oreille, while the Coeur d'Alene lived farther south around the lake country. These groups of Kutenai, Kalispel, and Coeur d'Alene seldom traveled into central or southern Idaho, and they had little contact with the Shoshoni. Northern Paiute, though, did have contact with the Shoshoni; they roamed through what we know as southwestern Idaho, occasionally venturing north of the Snake River in family or small band groups. Sheepeaters, an isolated group of Mountain Shoshoni, were scattered in the mountains south of the Salmon River and on the upper part of the Snake River.[2]

The origins of the Northern Paiute and Shoshoni are not known, although records show they have similar cultures to those Indians of the Great Basin and the Great Plains.[3] Scholars dispute the linguistic details of Uto-Aztecan languages, one of which the Weisers spoke, but Sven Liljeblad, an authority on these languages, feels there was no difference in the speech of the Weisers and other Shoshoni groups. When these Shoshoni groups migrated into the Snake River country, they continued their traditional subsistence life-style as hunters and gatherers, moving up and down the rivers and streams in search of roots, seeds, and small game.

By the 1800s, the migrations of Shoshoni people had spread over much of Nevada and into Wyoming. Northern Shoshoni people had been entrenched for generations in the Snake River country, while Sheepeater groups occupied the Salmon River Mountains of what is now southern Idaho and were scattered eastward into the Yellowstone country and the Wind River Mountains. Before 1780, the Shoshoni had even extended from the plains of Alberta and Saskatchewan to Texas, but disease and warfare forced them to retreat to the confines of the Rocky Mountains. Southern Shoshoni peoples not only occupied the lands as far south as Death Valley and Utah Lake, but the Comanche—a Shoshoni band of the southern plains—had extended into Texas and New Mexico.[4]

Thus, the Nez Perce, Northern Paiute, and Northern Shoshoni represent the historic peoples of the Weiser and Payette area. The isolated mountainous country lies to the west and north of present-day Boise between the Payette drainage on the east and the Snake River boundary with Oregon on the west.[5]

The Snake River area at the confluences of the Boise, Payette, and Weiser rivers was used primarily by the Boise Shoshoni, a major band with horses, but was shared peacefully by others. The buffalo-hunting Bannock, a Northern Paiute band who were also mounted and who eventually merged with the Northern Shoshoni, visited the area in their travels, using the opportunity to join in fishing for salmon.[6] The lower Payette country was also used by a few Northern Paiute who penetrated the sagebrush plains along the Snake River. They roamed the arid land in a constant search for food, moving nearly every day and seldom venturing into the mountains to the north.[7] They preferred the mild winters of the lower valleys where they had access to roots, seeds, crickets, rodents, and small game. These Northern Paiute had a winter village on the downstream stretches of Payette Valley. Unlike their relatives to the south in Nevada and to the west in Oregon, this Paiute group was fortunate in having abundant root crops and salmon on which to depend. They interacted freely with the Shoshoni peoples and there was no recognized boundary between the two cultures.

It has been in the recent historic past that the Mountain Shoshoni—of which the Weisers are one group—began to occupy the upper Weiser and Payette country. The archeological record is incomplete, but it indicates there was only light use of the area by earlier peoples.[8] The Weiser Shoshoni moved into

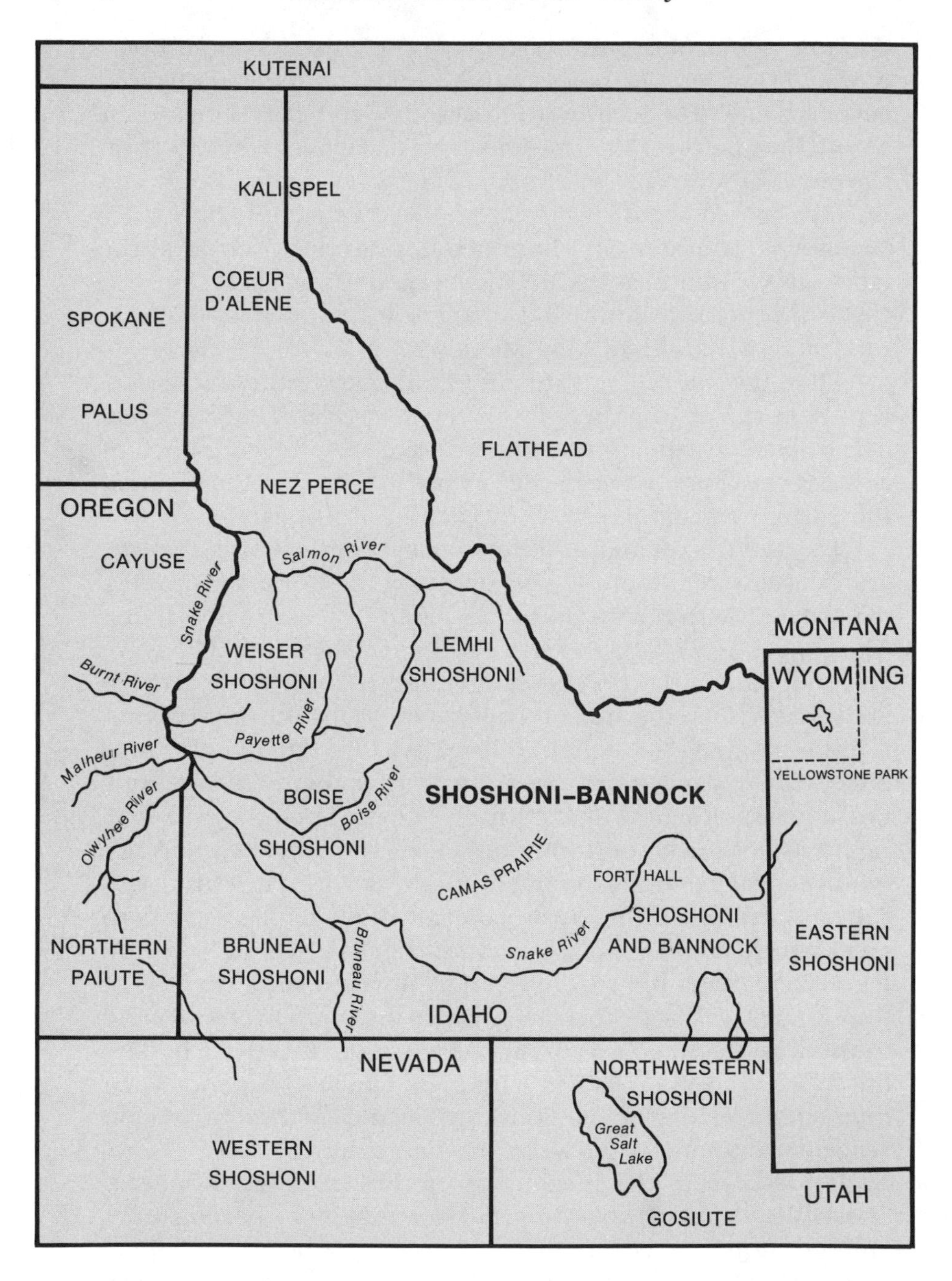

Homelands of the Northern Shoshoni, 1863.

the high valleys of the upper Weiser River and utilized the country from the lower Hells Canyon area, east to the Middle Fork country. Their summer camps were scattered throughout the mountainous area of the Payette and the country around the South Fork of the Salmon River.

Although there was little trouble with the friendly Paiute bands to the south, the Nez Perce who frequented the same country were hostile toward the Weisers. When another Shoshoni group attempted to locate a village in the deepest part of Hells Canyon at Battle Creek, on the Oregon side, the Nez Perce destroyed it. However, the undeclared state of war and antagonism between the Nez Perce and the Shoshoni has been exaggerated. In fact, the Weiser Shoshoni intermarried with and were closely aligned with several of the Nez Perce bands frequenting their area. The Weiser Shoshoni had little use for war with other native groups, and their valleys became a place of trade and peace for the Basin and Plateau peoples, as well as for others throughout the West.[9]

The meaning of the term "Shoshoni" has been lost. The Shoshoni were called "Snakes" by the Indians of the Great Plains, because they painted snakes on sticks to frighten their enemies. White explorers, unable—or uncaring—to differentiate between the peoples they encountered, later used the name "Snakes" for Shoshoni and Paiute.[10]

The various Shoshoni groups referred to themselves after the food source they were exploiting in a given locality. If they happened to be fishing for salmon, they might have been called salmon eaters (*aqaideka*) or, if hunting buffalo, they might refer to themselves as buffalo eaters (*kutsundeka*). This was confusing due to the high mobility of groups and families when they traveled from one food source to another during the year. The Weiser people would often refer to themselves as mountain sheep eaters (*tukedeka*) when hunting sheep in Hells Canyon or when visiting or hunting with other Sheepeaters of the Middle Fork country. Still another food source name for the Weiser Shoshoni was driftwood salmon eaters (*wobiaqvideka*), derived from the salmon's habit of lying under driftwood in small streams.[11]

Another, and more useful way—to the whites—of distinguishing the separate groups, was by use of a peculiar trait or geographical feature. The White Knives (Tossawihi) of the Bruneau country took their name from the white flint knives they carried, while the Sage Brush Knoll People (Puhugwe) referred to the people located near the present site of Fort Hall. *Seewooki*, a place-name originating with early trappers, designated the great bend of the Snake River and eventually applied to the Shoshoni-speaking populations on the lower Boise, Owyhee, Malheur, Payette, and Weiser rivers. Seewooki, a Shoshoni term, referred to the wooded countryside and was especially used to denote the people and country of the Weiser River.[12] I cannot say whether it was whites or Indians who designated the groups after traits or geographic features. Probably it was a little of both and could only be determined on a case by case basis. Since the names are of native origin, I am assuming the majority of times it was by Indian groups identifying other populations in other areas. The names are historical, from early records, and I am sure that in most cases the origins have been lost.

White people who later came into the country often substituted these traditional names with their own. Such was the case with the Sheepeater population in eastern Idaho, the Lemhis, whose winter camps were in the Lemhi Valley.[13] They were given the name because early Mormon settlers there referred to *Limhi*, a king in the Book of Mormon.

The Weiser Shoshoni were another Sheepeater (Mountain Shoshoni) group given their name by the early whites who encountered them on the river where the Indians made their winter camps. *Weiser* is not a native name. It is taken from Peter Weiser (Wizer or Wiser), a member of the Lewis and Clark Expedition, and was being used by trappers as early as 1812.[14]

Historically, the term "Weisers" has referred to those Mountain Shoshoni and Indian peoples who occupied the upper Weiser River area near the present towns of Council and Indian Valley. In early literature they were referred to as a "mixed band" or the "Weiser Indians." As all Shoshoni peoples did, these Indians simply called themselves "the people."[15]

Originally, the Weiser group of Mountain Shoshoni were often confused with other Sheepeaters of the Salmon River Mountains. As far as is known, they spoke the same dialect as these more traditional kinsmen, and there appears to be no linguistic difference in their speech. The Sheepeater populations along the rugged Middle Fork of the Salmon River were isolated from the other Northern Shoshoni groups located further south and were noted for the retention of an older "slow singsong speech" pattern.[16]

The Weisers—and their kinsmen—lived a nomadic existence, roaming the mountains and high valleys. They lacked territorial and political unity, preferring instead to remain in independent families or small groups. They were noted furriers and skilled craftsmen, who had tailored garments of the finest skins long before the Plains Indians, and their bows of mountain-sheep horn were highly prized throughout the West.[17]

These mountain Indians, the Weisers and other Sheepeaters, differed from the major Shoshoni groups in several ways. They inhabited areas where salmon could be taken, and so salmon, rather than antelope and bison, became their major food source. Further, although the population scattered to different fishing sites, the yearly salmon runs allowed a period in which a stable residence within a small village was possible. Most other Shoshoni groups had no such stability.[18]

But the Weisers were different in another, important way from most other Shoshoni: As they moved up and down the streams of Idaho's western mountains, they came into contact with the Plateau culture of the Nez Perce of the lower Salmon River. These Nez Perce neighbors lived in permanent winter villages, and were nomadic only in the summer. The peaceful but modest form of trade that ensued promoted a cultural exchange between the two peoples that left a significant mark on the Weisers.[19]

The Plateau culture was based on salmon fishing and camas digging in the early days, and the Weisers incorporated these and other elements into their own life-style. They found roots abundant, especially around the present city of Weiser; food was plentiful in the mountain valleys; and thus, they lived well before the coming of the white man.[20]

Woven mat lodges such as this were all but abandoned in favor of the conical hide tipis adopted from the Great Plains culture. (Courtesy of Oregon Historical Society, neg. no. OrHi 4466)

SUBSISTENCE ACTIVITIES

The Weisers established their semipermanent winter camps in the lush upper valleys of the Weiser River where they found the winters mild. In these camps, they built conical pole lodges thatched with woven mats or bundled grass and had sweat houses and menstrual huts. Typically, Shoshoni villages could accommodate fifteen to twenty families and were centrally located among their food sources. The mild winter temperatures, availability of stored foods, water, and sufficient wood for fuel and shelters made ideal conditions for these winter village encampments.[21]

During the early spring and summer months individual families or small groups left the winter village to establish temporary camps. Thus began a migratory cycle of food gathering activities, or seasonal rounds. Some groups or single families journeyed into the high mountains to hunt large game, and others traveled to the favorite fishing locations. The Weisers—and their neighbors, the Northern Paiute of eastern Oregon—took salmon from the Boise, Weiser, Payette, and Snake rivers, all major fish runs.[22] Steelhead arrived during April's high water in all forks and tributaries of these rivers, including Squaw Creek, and the Chinook came in September. "They were speared, caught in nets, or trapped by means of weirs."[23] Because there were no falls to form a natural fishing place in the larger rivers, the Weisers constructed barriers of stones or brush to force the fish into certain places where they could be easily taken. Red salmon (sockeye) ran in vast numbers between August and late October and spawned in Big Payette Lake. The river outlet on Payette Lake was one of the favorite summer camps of the Weiser Shoshoni and Nez Perce of the lower Salmon River. Other Sheepeater groups traveled over the mountains to join them at the lake for communal hunting and fishing.[24]

Pine grass, elksedge, snowberry, bitterbrush, huckleberry, chokecherry, serviceberry, currants, balsam root, lupine, and Solomon's seal were common to the Weiser and Payette areas, and there was camas in the wet meadows of the higher elevations from Smiths Ferry, north through Long Valley, and into Salmon Meadows. The Shoshoni could have exploited well over one hundred different types of plants. There were large herds of mule deer and elk, along with black bear, beaver, martin, mink, and otter. Bald eagles, golden eagles, grouse, geese, ducks, and hawks of various kinds were abundant, and the Weisers hunted mountain sheep, mountain goats, and other large game in the Salmon River area and the Seven Devils Mountains.[25]

In the prehorse period the Weisers depended on small game such as porcupine, cottontail, jackrabbit, rock chucks, badger, and rodents as sources of meat and protein. They also caught frogs and ants, gathered larvae of various insects, and collected birds' eggs. Rock chucks, crickets, and grasshoppers were considered special delicacies; they roasted the larger grasshoppers and formed the rest into cakes for winter storage.[26]

Hunting ducks, geese, and other waterfowl, like fishing, was a communal affair in which everyone might participate, but big game hunting was left to the men. It was the women who, besides hunting small game, harvested the plants, dried fish, and prepared foods for winter storage. The men hunted individually or in small groups, often with dogs trained for the chase. Whatever game was taken was always divided with the other hunters and their families, but the hide went to the one who made the kill. The women dressed the skins into white, yellow, and brown buckskins of the highest quality.[27]

There were festivals at least once a year, and sometimes two or three times a year. For the Weisers and their friends, these celebrations were periods of gathering. They were arranged when there were sufficient food supplies on hand to support large numbers of people for five days or so. As social events, the festivals marked a renewal of friendships and strengthened family ties. Also, they were fun: There were games, gambling, foot races, and trading; and, in addition, there were ceremonial dances.[28]

The rules of social behavior were complicated. Marriage, kinship relations, and the function of the extended family formed the frame for all activity and the economy at large.[29] But, like their Nez Perce neighbors, the Weisers did not have much in the way of tribal unity before the arrival of the white man.

Like many other Shoshoni groups, the true political unit of the Weisers was the village, a small and variable group, with the family being the maximum economic unit. One family, or group of related families, was the basic sociopolitical entity, with both the social and political control limited to a small group of members. This unit, related by blood, together with spouses who married into the group, formed what is today called a ***kindred***. Any larger groupings for social and economic purposes were temporary and shifting.[30]

The extended family group, under the guidance of the more experienced family heads, practiced a democratic form of leadership. Membership in the village group, or kindred, was never entirely stable, and people would come and go for various reasons.[31] Since the Weisers were not a fixed political unit under an autocratic chief, they were tolerant of flexibility and cooperation.

Individual leaders, or talkers (*tegwani*), among the Weisers were men of experience, not necessarily aged, and their primary task was to keep informed about the ripening plant foods and good hunting areas. This talker gave "long orations, telling of his information and giving directions to families who cared to cooperate. His authority was not absolute. Any family was at liberty to pursue an independent course at any time."[32] These leaders, or headmen, were usually men of wealth or good judgment, and had a degree of influence in communal affairs. Their authority, however, was "restricted to leadership in hunting and in warfare and later also in dealing with the white man and his government."[33]

Late fall marked the end of the Weisers' seasonal rounds and was a time of intensive preparation for winter. The meats, fish, and various plant foods that had been prepared throughout the summer were brought in to be cached in dry, protected areas near the winter camp. The Weisers' storage containers were constructed of a highly developed basketry technique, and the pottery was made from a claylike soil found along the Bruneau River.[34]

During the winter days, the Weisers chipped arrowheads and made knives and skin scrapers from obsidian taken from Timber Butte near Squaw Creek. The women cooked, gathered wood, and tanned hides for making garments and robes. The upper Weiser country was prime winter range for deer and elk, so the Weisers hunted year round, though from December to February there was limited activity.[35] If the winter was unusually long or harsh, the Weisers would sometimes be in a near-starving condition as supplies dwindled or ran out.

A CHANGING LIFE-STYLE

Within white man's history, there were three things that radically altered the Indians' way of life: guns, liquor, and horses. The most important of these was the horse, which was introduced around 1750, when Comanches living in the Southwest obtained them from nearby Spanish settlements. In turn, the horses were passed on to other Shoshoni and Plains Indians, and to the Plateau people to the north. The Nez Perce got horses from the Plains Indians, and from these eastern tribes they learned an entire complex of techniques and ideas centered around bison hunting.[36]

While many Shoshoni were quick to adopt this new life of plenty, the effects were not uniform, and some of the Shoshoni, notably the Sheepeaters, retained many of the old ways. Although not all Shoshoni groups who adopted the horse were equally affected, in most cases the changes were revolutionary. Fundamental changes in activities and practices caused the Northern Shoshoni to depart radically from the Western Shoshoni peoples to the south. Thus, the major division of the Shoshoni nation into Northern and Western is cultural as well as geographic. The latter held to the original way of life, while the Northern Shoshoni were heavily influenced by the peoples of the Plains and Plateau.[37]

An even sharper division of cultural traits was adopted by the Eastern Shoshoni of Idaho and Wyoming, who became buffalo hunters. The evolution to a people with horses and a buffalo-based economy included "such novel ideas as living in tipis; jerking meat in large quantities, wearing neatly tailored and ornamented skin clothing, feather headdresses at festive occasions, and war decoration; [and] practicing certain ceremonial dances of Plains origin."[38]

The Indians now known as Boise, Fort Hall, and Lemhi Shoshoni in eastern Idaho were transformed into mounted buffalo hunters and warriors on a similar, but more modest, scale. The migratory life-style was appealing, but because of the danger in traveling beyond their old habitats, they banded together in larger groups and began to recognize regular leaders. These band leaders—more or less equal in prominence—guided buffalo expeditions beyond the mountains and led the others into battle against their enemies. Mounted groups of Northern Paiute, to the west in Oregon and Nevada, were quick to join and travel with these Shoshoni and emerged as the Bannock Indians of Idaho.[39]

The horse had a major impact on the Weiser Shoshoni in several ways. Although a "band" organization in the anthropological and classical sense was lacking among these people, the horse permitted a loose form of social development; large groups of people could come together and bring their foods to a central point.[40] The ecology supported the development of a horse-based culture. The Weisers found the valleys of the upper Payette and Weiser country to be well suited for horses. The hills were covered with bunchgrass and the bottomlands furnished rye grass throughout the winter months, even when the snow was deep.[41]

Becoming more mobile in their seasonal rounds, the Weisers' travels expanded, even though they still preferred their mountain life-style over the Plains concept. Individual families might have joined occasionally with other mounted groups to hunt buffalo far to the east, but as a cluster of interrelated families, the Weiser group had no need or desire to leave their mountain country.[42]

The horse not only allowed the Weiser Shoshoni to hunt big game more often, but permitted them to travel to such distant locations as Stanley Basin, the Seven Devils Mountains, and the Salmon River country to hunt, fish, or harvest camas. Their dependence on small game diminished with the expansion of their more mobile life-style. The adoption of hide lodges allowed whole camps to relocate easily, and they began to abandon their traditional grass lodges. Yet they would resort to them on occasion in times of emergency, or for temporary camps when they were away from the main village.[43]

Although other independent Sheepeater groups in what is now central Idaho remained isolated until recent times, the Weisers had frequent contact with their neighbors. The ancient Nez Perce Indian trail into the Snake River country came by way of the Seven Devils, crossed over the mountains, and wound down into the Weiser River drainage.[44] The horse brought not only the Nez Perce, but also the Spokanes, Flatheads, Cayuse, and other tribes of the Northwest into the Weiser country.

There is, at present, no way to place a set number of years on the occupation of the area by Weiser Shoshoni. Almost no archeological work has been done to date, and the record is unclear. However, some interesting finds have been made by Max Pavesic, of Boise State University, that include a burial complex and a 5,000-year-old tool-making site. But as he told me, only the surface has been scratched so far, and many years of extensive fieldwork will have to be completed before a clear record will exist on native occupation of the area.

Food surpluses, such as salmon and the localized abundance of camas in the Snake River region, provided for the growth of a well-developed trading area. The valley where the Boise, Owyhee, Malheur, Payette, and Weiser rivers joined the Snake became a great "Peace Valley" in the Indian world. A legendary fair, or salmon festival, was a yearly intertribal gathering, or rendezvous, held early in the summer. It would last for a month or more. Different tribes and bands from throughout the West would meet without fear in order to trade or make treaties and to celebrate the beginning of the fishing. The Bannock would come to barter for salmon; the Nez Perce brought fine horses to trade; the Umatilla and Cayuse were intermediaries for Pacific Coast ornamental seashells; even Cheyenne and Arapaho bands came, dragging their superior tipi poles made from Colorado cedar. Sheepeater groups brought quality skins and tanned hides, while the Northern Paiute had finely chipped obsidian arrowheads to offer. Only two other locations in the entire Northwest could compare in scope to this trade center: The Dalles on the Columbia in Oregon and the Mandan villages on the Missouri in North Dakota.[45]

The social and cultural changes brought about by the introduction of the horse were rapid and had a far-reaching impact, not only on the Weiser Sheepeaters, but on all the Northern Shoshoni in general. "During this brief and final period of tribal independence, the Idaho Indians experienced a life of plenty as never before and never since."[46]

TWO

The First White Men

THE FUR TRAPPERS

The beginning of the historic period in Idaho dates from 1805 with the arrival of the Lewis and Clark Expedition in the Lemhi country, in what would eventually become eastern Idaho, and their subsequent journey westward across the northern portion of the state. This is the period when the archeological record merges with that of written history.[1] When these early explorers reached the Lemhi peoples, Lewis consulted with a Boise Shoshoni informant who suggested traveling down the unexplored Snake River after waiting until spring for better travel conditions. Uncertain whether he was being directed to a Columbia or lower Colorado destination, Lewis feared to adopt such a route. It is probable that his "Broken Moccasins," a people of which he learned that lived to the west in the Salmon River Mountains, were the elusive Sheepeater people.[2]

The Lewis and Clark Expedition made several attempts to penetrate the Salmon country during their brief visit in Idaho. From Lemhi they struggled to find a way through the canyon of the Salmon River, but were forced to turn back and take a northern route through the Nez Perce country. While visiting with the Nez Perce, a small party that included Peter Weiser was sent south toward Hells Canyon after salmon. The party found a "high broken mountainous country generally well timbered with . . . an abundance of deer and some bighorned animals."[3] They were still forty miles from Weiser's river, as it came to be known by 1812, but they had come close to that area.

On the heels of these explorers, in the 1820s and 1830s, came the "romantic and adventurous era of the fur trade. Within two or three decades the beaver hunters had overrun the entire un-

Donald Mackenzie. (Courtesy of Idaho State Historical Society)

known territory"[4] just at the time when the Indian peoples in Idaho had reached their Golden Age. These exploration and trapping expeditions left a great amount of knowledge of their activities while in the Weiser country, and gave us the first written records documenting an earlier history of Shoshonean culture.

But the first expedition to cross southern Idaho and reach the Weiser River was the ill-fated Astoria party, led by Wilson Price Hunt in 1811. The Hunt party's harrowing, eleven-month adventure is one of the sagas in Northwest history. The party endured starvation and hardship in the "Snake Country" before reaching Astoria on the Columbia.[5] A canoe accident forced the party to divide into three groups, and each group made its way separately across southern Idaho. One of these groups was led by Donald Mackenzie,[6] who hurried ahead, taking a general northwest course from Caldron Linn, a dangerous rapid on the Snake River where their canoes overturned and a number of the party drowned. The group led by Hunt traveled down the north side of the Snake, while a third party, led by a veteran trapper named Ramsay Crooks, followed along the south bank. Only occasional relief could be obtained by the explorers at the few scattered Indian encampments, and these Indians had little to share with the white strangers.

The group led by Mackenzie reached the Weiser River and crossed it on November 28, 1811, but found their way west blocked by the impenetrable gorge of Hells Canyon. Although it was late fall, they headed north over the Seven Devils Mountains on what is considered "one of the most daring pathfinder trips in the history of the Northwest."[7] The exact movements of Mackenzie's party are shrouded in mystery, but he eventually led the group to the source of the Weiser River. Following an Indian trail, later known as the Old Boise Trail, Mackenzie crossed the lower Salmon and continued north toward present-day Lewiston. After twenty-one days Mackenzie's group reached the Clearwater River.[8] Thus, he is credited with being the first white man to traverse the Weiser country.

After crossing the Weiser River, Hunt and his group found themselves barred by the mountains of Hells Canyon and they were forced to turn back. Reaching the lower Weiser once again, they came across a dozen lodges of Shoshoni who had recently arrived. The Shoshoni informed Hunt of the impossibility of going through the canyon. Hearing this, Hunt decided to leave the main route and proceeded up Weiser Valley. "Some distance up this stream"[9] he found another encampment of friendly Shoshoni who shared their meager winter supplies with the destitute party. He was able to procure "a couple of horses, a dog, a few dried fish, and some roots and dried cherries," but was unable to get the Indians to guide his party over the mountains. They told him the snow was waist deep and replied, "We shall freeze! We shall freeze!"[10] They urged him to stay and spend the winter with the village.

Without a guide Hunt knew his party could never find its way through the mountains. He charged this group of Shoshoni with talking with a "forked tongue," and challenged their courage by calling them women. At length he was able to induce one of the Indians to volunteer as a guide.[11] After he had stayed with these Shoshoni until December 21, he returned down the Weiser to the Snake.[12] The Shoshoni guide bravely returned with him down the Weiser, taking him back to the Snake River. This Indian guide then stayed with them, suffering alongside them through hunger and exhaustion. He led the entire party over the Blue Mountains of Oregon, in the middle of winter, and eventually brought them safely down to the Umatilla River, and to the Columbia. Crossing the river, he reunited with Crook's party and made his way to Astoria, on the Oregon coast, where he found Mackenzie's group waiting for him.

Hunt left six men on the Weiser. These men chose to remain among the Snakes rather than risk a winter crossing of the mountains to the Columbia.[13] They were fortunate that the Shoshoni did not molest them. Some of the horses Hunt had taken had been stolen when they could not be gained through trade. The Indians, however, had never seen white men and had a superstitious feeling regarding them. Although the Shoshoni would "encamp near them in the daytime, they would move off with their tents in the night; and finally disappeared, without taking leave."[14]

The Hunt Expedition made the region known to the outside world. Mackenzie, in particular, had noted that the mountain streams were alive with beaver, and his estimations would prove correct: the Weiser, Payette, and Boise rivers would prove to be the premier beaver streams in Idaho.[15]

In 1813, a party of trappers under John Reid, who had been with the Mackenzie party, returned from Astoria to what would be known as the Boise River and built a rude cabin and corral near its mouth. Reid intended to "pass the winter in the Snake country, collect the stragglers still wandering through that quarter"[16] and rejoin the main party the following spring. Early in 1814, Reid and his men were massacred by a band of "Dog-Rib" Snakes who were later identified as Bannocks. The only survivors were Marie Dorian, an Indian woman married to one of the trappers, and her two children, who made a heroic journey back to Astoria with the tragic news.[17]

The setback for the whites was only temporary. During the next few years, trappers and explorers were filtering into Shoshoni country from the north and east, but plans were also under way to invade it from the west.[18] Mackenzie returned in the fall of 1818, leading the first Snake River Expedition of the North West Company, a rival Canadian franchise of the Hudson's Bay Company, that consisted of "55 men, 195 horses and 300 beaver traps besides a considerable stock of merchandise."[19] Among the veteran trappers employed by the North West Company were French-Canadians, Iroquois Indians, and half bloods, complete with tipis, dogs, children, and women. Unlike the Americans, the British had decided to travel in large bodies for mutual protection as they moved from one beaver stream to another.[20]

The Indian people of southern Idaho greatly interested Mackenzie, and as he studied them, he arrived at some interesting conclusions in regards to the fur trade. Unlike Indians in the north and east, these mountain Indians did not enjoy trapping, which they termed "women's work," and were unwilling to give up their life-styles. If furs were to be obtained, the companies would have to do it themselves and not just rely on an improvised trade network with the natives.[21]

An even more serious problem existed that regarded warfare between the natives. Mackenzie was aware that Blackfoot war parties from the plains penetrated the Snake country, striking deep into the Shoshoni heartland in search of plunder and horses. To make matters worse, the Nez Perce and other Sahaptin-speaking peoples to the north and west often were at war with the Snake bands. The danger and attacks posed by both sides could disrupt any future trapping expeditions. Before leaving the Columbia, Mackenzie had met with the Nez Perce headmen in a round of councils and convinced them to agree to a peace, providing the Snake bands agreed.[22] The establishment of friendly relations between the native peoples of the region became one of his paramount objectives while trapping the Snake country.

Reaching the Boise valley, Mackenzie dropped off the Iroquois with instructions to trap the Boise, Payette, and Weiser rivers. He hoped they would be able to set good examples of such activity while he delivered Nez Perce peace messages along the Snake. Upon his return, he found the Iroquois trappers had "abandoned themselves with the savages and were doing nothing."[23] In disgust at losing his veteran trappers, he left and returned to his headquarters on the Columbia.

The following year, 1819, Mackenzie returned to the Boise Valley on a second Snake expedition and held the first trappers' rendezvous. He began building a permanent post near the site of the John Reid massacre, but soon abandoned the idea after two of his men were killed. Later, a group of Bannocks tried to storm his camp in a harrowing adventure,[24] while he was waiting for his party to assemble.

Alexander Ross, chronicler for the Mackenzie expedition, tried to divide the "great Snake nation" into three divisions: the "dog-eaters" (Shirry-dikas),[25] who were the buffalo hunters of the plains; the "fish-eaters" (War-are-ree-kas); and the Bannocks (Ban-at-tees), or "mountain Snakes." These large composite bands were actually made up of what came to be known as the Boise, Fort Hall, and many smaller bands of Northern Shoshoni who had joined together for protection from their enemies.

In the spring of 1820, Mackenzie met in a grand council on Little Lost River with the large band of Boise Shoshoni led by Big Jim (Chief Peiem). Mackenzie and the Shoshoni reached an agreement to let his fur-trapping enterprise operate.[26] Peiem (the Shoshoni word for "Big Jim") and an Arapaho (War-are-ree-ka) chief, Amaketsa, assured peace. But, they told the trappers, the Bannocks were impossible to control and were "a preditory [*sic*] race, and the chief cause of all the Snake trouble with the Nez Perces."[27] Still, Mackenzie continued his peace efforts while he was in the area, and when he left in 1821, Nez Perce and Shoshoni parties were meeting not only in the Weiser and Boise countries, but in villages all across southern Idaho. As Mackenzie had foreseen, the peace proved beneficial for all the parties involved. The Nez Perce traded for the furs that the Shoshoni trapped in the mountain streams and, as middlemen, were bringing the furs to the British trading posts on the Columbia.[28] It is evident that the Indian attitude toward trapping, which earlier had been women's work, must have changed, or that at least a sizable portion of the Shoshoni began to trap. This was probably due to the influx of white trade goods—valuable items that they found could be exchanged for easily obtained skins.

The Hudson's Bay Company assumed control of the trapping expeditions after Mackenzie's departure. Alexander Ross led the 1824 excursion into Idaho, where he "began a difficult trapping and exploring course" through the Weiser country.[29] On Reid's (Boise) River he encountered Peiem and his band, who were en route to visit Amaketsa on the Weiser and who had stopped to hold council with a Nez Perce peace delegation. After passing down the Boise River, Ross and his trappers reached the Payette, or "Middle River," and traveled up its course 110 miles to cross over "some thirty miles" where they "fell on River Weiser":[30]

> As a fishing place on the Wuzer (Weiser) River Ross estimated a camp of War-are-reekas under Chief Ama-Ketsa to have 900 tents, 4,500 (a great exaggeration) persons, and half that many horses. They were gambling, fishing, and sporting; they had few guns.[31]

The arrival of American competition into the fur trade created new problems for both the British and the Indians and the Americans were not welcomed by either. Where an uneasy peace prevailed with the Hudson's Bay white men, the Shoshoni now found their country being overrun by the "Long Knives" of the Rocky Mountain Fur Company. By the spring of 1826, the Americans had penetrated deep into the Weiser country and had trapped all the way to the Payette Lakes.[32]

The British expeditions from 1825 to 1830 into southern Idaho were led by Peter Skene Ogden, who had taken over the leadership of the Snake expeditions in 1824 upon merger of the North West Company and Hudson's Bay Company. Ogden's well-kept records of Shoshoni contacts during the height of the fur trade have proved invaluable to historians. In 1827, while trapping the "Wayer's River" (Weiser), he noted the intrusion of the Americans when he found a party of forty trappers with a band of Nez Perce working the area: "The trappers were in every direction in quest of beaver. The Americans will not part with one." Pushing on to the Boise River, Ogden wrote in disgust: "I have little hope as the American trappers are everywhere. . . . It was from the Wazer's, Payette's and this river we expected our returns."[33] That the rich beaver country was being trapped out was of little consequence to the Hudson's Bay Company. Hoping to create a beaver-barren zone, they were pursuing a "scorched-earth policy" in the hopes of keeping the Americans out of the British Northwest.[34]

The furs began to diminish and the trappers suffered from Indian attacks. Thanks to Mackenzie's earlier peace efforts, the British were protected from most of the depredations committed by the Bannock, but the Americans were not. Ogden stated that in the three years following 1823, no less than thirty-two Americans had been killed in the Snake country. But neither the Americans, the British, nor the Shoshoni had much protection against the Blackfeet war parties. From Camas Prairie west to the Owyhee country, the British trappers reported widespread attacks by these raiders.[35]

John Work, Ogden's successor as leader of the Hudson's Bay Company's annual Snake expedition, was on the Weiser in September 1830, where he found "a few Snake Indians" encamped. From these he learned, much to his relief, that "the great Snake camp is off to the Buffaloe." The advantage of this, he wrote, was that "they will be before us and amuse the Blackfeet." He stopped long enough to send a party of six men northward "where they are to hunt on the upper parts of Waser and Payette's Rivers and to cross the Mountains on some of the branches of the Salmon river."[36]

In 1831, a band of mountain men of the American Fur Company reached Stanley Basin. Obtaining an Indian guide who knew the country, they traveled into Bear Valley, crossed the upper South Fork of the Salmon, and reached Long Valley on the Payette. What their guide showed these men, however, was not beaver, but a fabulous elk herd, much to their disappointment. They returned, convinced of the futility of further exploration for beaver in the Salmon River Mountains.[37]

By the time Captain Benjamin L. E. Bonneville, an officer on leave from the U.S. Army, arrived in the Weiser area in 1832, he had already noticed the seasonal food gathering rounds followed by large bands of migratory Indians he met. The Bannocks, early in the spring, moved down the Snake River from the upper Snake River plains to camp on the Boise and Payette rivers where they found good hunting and pasture. The Indians continued down the river to the Nez Perce of the Weiser area to trade beaver and buffalo robes for horses.[38]

At the mouth of the Little Weiser, Bonneville met some Shoshoni who had come up from the Boise River plains earlier with horses and good equipment they had obtained from the lower Nez Perce. After being informed by his scouts that formidable bands of Bannocks were in the mountains, he pressed on into Oregon.

A TIME OF PEACE

By 1834, the Hudson's Bay Company had established a post on the lower Snake River. Known as "Snake Fort," it was moved in 1836 to a permanent location near the mouth of the Boise River and placed in charge of its new postmaster, François Payette. With the decline in the fur trade, it became more important as a trading post than as a fur center and was the only permanent trading center between Fort Hall, purchased by the Company in 1836, and the Columbia.[39] The Mountain Shoshoni could still get "the guns and kettles which the white men had introduced and which had become so essential to a new Indian way of life."[40]

The lasting effects of the fur trade did more than make the Shoshoni bands dependent on white goods.[41] This trade led to a decline in power for many of the Northern Shoshoni. While the Eastern Shoshoni and Lemhi were forced to remain in large composite bands in order to compete with enemies in the buffalo country, the powerful Boise band under noted Chief Peiem, and the Bannocks led by The Horse (also known as "The Horn Chief") began to break into smaller, more independent groups once again. The Blackfeet posed less of a threat since their advance had been effectively halted through war and disease, and their war parties now seldom ventured into central or southern Idaho. The Shoshoni and Bannock bands of the lower Snake could pursue their traditional life-style and still meet in peace with the Nez Perce and other Plateau Indians in the trading center of the Boise, Payette, and Weiser valleys.

By the arrival of the 1840s, beaver prices in the East went into decline, as the demand dropped. The independent mountain men and smaller trapping companies in the West began to retire. With the departure of the fur trappers from the Weiser scene, the mountain country north of the Snake River returned to its isolated character, and the small groups and bands of Indians lived peacefully in their mountain domain. Occasionally, small parties of trappers working under the direction of François Payette would pass through the area, but the disruption to the Mountain Shoshoni life-style was minimal.[42]

The Weiser Shoshoni remained in their isolated existence in mountain valleys during this time, and there is no record of the group being located elsewhere. They were not well organized into one social or political group,[43] but, for the most part, came together as individual families at favorite camping areas. Without white interference they were free to scatter throughout the mountains during the summer in order to hunt and fish along the branches of the Payette and Weiser rivers, and to visit their favorite fishing and hunting sites at the Payette Lakes and on the South Fork of the Salmon River.

Though the records indicate that the Mountain Shoshoni seldom ventured far from their homeland, they did travel for trade. Cutting across the mountains by way of Stanley Basin, some of the mountain people would undertake the journey to Camas Prairie, in south-central Idaho, where Indians of western Idaho and bands from the upper Snake country congregated to harvest camas and socialize.[44] The trip was hazardous, and they sometimes fell prey to other groups who robbed them of their trade goods along the route.

Mountain Shoshoni also visited Boise Valley to trade with their Indian friends and probably stopped at the Snake Fort run by the French-Canadian Payette, who had trapped their country since the beginning of the fur trade and who was described as a "kind and polite man."[45] These trips to the lower country were kept to a minimum according to the lack of entries in the official records, and it is well known that the Weisers rarely visited the whites.[46]

The Indians in the lower valleys along the Snake also enjoyed peaceful conditions for the decade following the diminishing of the fur trade. With the extinction of the buffalo on the Snake River plains, many of the small bands who had horses would still come together and join with the larger Shoshoni bands to the east in order to hunt on the Great Plains.[47] But the Weisers were content to live their independent and traditional life-style.

The Weisers and their neighbors were fortunate to be spared the often confusing and bitter divisions that developed within the western tribes, due to the activities and rivalries among the different faiths and clergymen. White influence and values from the eastern missionaries soon spread through the Plateau peoples of the Northwest, eventually leading to much unrest and finally to war.

In October 1840, the last link of the Oregon Trail had been forged when a group of trappers and their Indian families left Fort Boise—the new, permanent location of what had been called Snake Fork—with wagons and reached the Columbia River over the old Indian and pack trail. This feat, coupled with the glowing accounts of rich lands on the Oregon frontier, was the signal that permanent white settlement had come to the Oregon country.[48]

THE TURMOIL BEGINS

By 1843, the great emigration to Oregon was under way. Thousands of settlers flocked to the new lands beyond the Blue Mountains. Cutting across the heart of the Northern Shoshoni country, the route followed the same course as that taken by the Astorians in 1811. The "horde of travelers brought a mixed blessing of grasslands denuded and food supplies curtailed but, at the same time, tremendous booty left along the road from overloaded wagons to crippled and worn-out cattle and horses" for the local Indians to recover.[49] It also brought the Indians into direct contact with a different type of white man, one less tolerant of Indian ways and one who found them to be a hindrance rather than an ally. It led to encounters on both sides that often proved disastrous.

But the Weiser Indians had a safe retreat. They had luxuriant forage for their horses in the upper Weiser and Payette valleys, and there was no contact with the emigrant parties to the south, whose cattle and horses depleted Indian grasslands.

The Shoshoni and Paiute of the lower valleys, whose territory was astride the Oregon Trail, suffered in different ways from emigrant trains. Those Indians with horses were in buffalo country hunting or in the mountains digging camas during the summer months when most of the emigrant traffic passed through en route to Oregon. When they returned in the fall, they found "burned-out campfires, denuded woodlands, and cropped-over pastures" in the wake of inconsiderate wagon trains.[50] At their favorite wintering areas, where they had kept the brush burned off for generations, they found only filthy campsites and streams fouled by the "white man's buffalo."

Those without horses, called "Diggers" by the emigrants because they lived a subsistence life-style there on the arid Snake River plains, had to watch their food sources destroyed by whites ignorant of Indian culture and blind to the delicate balance of the area's natural resources.

The Shoshoni and Paiute retaliated in the ways normal to them. Unable to rely upon their usual food sources, they took what they needed, stealing horses and killing livestock. The emigrants exaggerated the accounts of Indian robberies, and in their self-induced fear, often killed and punished innocent people.[51]

In 1846 Britain divided the Oregon country with the United States, but the governor of the new Provisional Territory of Oregon was unable to create any supervision for a growing Indian problem. In 1847 a wagon train infested with measles stopped at the Whitman Mission on the Columbia and the sickness infected the local Indians. The well-publicized massacre of the missionaries by the Indians which followed led to the Cayuse War and created unrest, suspicion, and a general distrust of all Indians in the territory.[52]

The situation around Fort Boise deteriorated rapidly after 1850, focusing some attention on the area by the newly created Oregon Superintendent of Indian Affairs.[53] In 1851 Superintendent of Indian Affairs Anson Dart and Governor John P. Gaines requested troops to keep check on the Snakes.

In August 1854, a band of Boise Shoshoni (Win-nes-tahs) wiped out the Ward party near Fort Boise. Only two of the party escaped; nineteen lost their lives in this most devastating attack ever committed by Indians in the Snake Country.[54] A military expedition led by Major Granville Haller arrived in the Boise Valley to subdue the Indians and to capture the offenders. Haller captured four Indians, but shot three of them when they broke and ran. Chief Oete and his band of Bannocks, who were visiting the fort, and who had nothing to do with the massacre, were given a stern lecture, but the Hudson's Bay employees reported Oete "as being a good Indian for the locality."[55] Two more Indians, presumably Shoshoni, were killed before the troops returned to their post at The Dalles.

The following April, Haller returned to chastise the guilty Indians. Special Agent Nathan Olney, of the Oregon Superintendent of Indian Affairs, accompanied him in order to compile a description of the native groups inhabiting the Snake country. They had a "talk" with several hundred Indians at the fort, where four more of the attackers had been taken prisoner. Three were later hanged at the massacre site, the fourth having been killed while attempting to escape.[56]

From the Boise River the troops headed east to Camas Prairie and Shoshone Falls while a smaller detachment was sent north to search the Salmon River area. Near the Salmon, four more Indians were killed. After a month of traversing the country in all directions, the expedition returned once again to The Dalles. Upon their departure from the Snake country, the British became concerned about the safety of manning the post on the Boise. The Ward incident had only highlighted the tense state of affairs and the post was abandoned in the autumn of 1855.[57]

Trying to manage the affairs of the Snake River Indians was no small chore for the Oregon superintendents, in spite of the fact that the Indians in eastern Idaho were now being managed by Utah territorial officials. Olney had concluded that the Snake bands numbered three thousand and of that number, three hundred were Sheepeaters (Too-koo-ree-keys).[58] Oregon officials regularly applied for funds to negotiate with the "Boonack, Snake and Mountain Snake tribes,"[59] but the agents were too far away to be of any effective use. The creation of Washington Territory only compounded the situation when, in 1857, the Oregon and Washington Territory superintendencies were combined under J. W. Nesmith. The Snake troubles were replaced in 1858 by an even bigger threat to peace in the Northwest with the outbreak of the Spokane War. It soon involved the Coeur d'Alene and Palouse tribes and threatened to engulf the entire Plateau region.[60]

The Indian hostility that continued to build in the Boise region did not go unnoticed by the people of Oregon. The Oregon legislature had already asked for troops to patrol the Immigrant Road in the Shoshoni country. In November 1858, Gen. William Harney of the Military Department of Oregon wrote his superiors:

> To secure the emigrant route to this department from the frontiers of Missouir [*sic*], I shall establish a post in the spring in the vicinity of Fort Boisee [*sic*], on Snake river, some two hundred and thirty miles from Fort Walla Walla.[61]

The Eastern Shoshoni under Gamblers Gourd (Chief Washakie) caused little trouble, for they had enough problems with their enemies on the Plains. Chiefs Foul Hand (Quintanian) and Snag (Tio-van-du-ah) managed to keep their Mountain Shoshoni in the Lemhi Valley quiet once they had driven a short-lived Mormon settlement out of their country and back to Utah. But the northwestern bands, led by chiefs Bear Hunter and Pocatello, continued to terrorize and commit depredations with alarming escalation in 1859.[62]

Ranging around the Boise and Camas Prairie areas were bands led by Buffalo-Meat-Under-the-Shoulder (Amaroko) and the Fort Boise Bannocks under Hairy Man (Poemacheah), both of whom had a large number of horses. Depredations in their areas along the Oregon Trail continued to intensify, in spite of the occasional appearance of army patrols. All of the hostile chiefs were under the influence of Sego Lily (Pasigo), a medicine man who was considered "a wonderful prophet by the Snakes."[63] It was this Bannock chief of Oregon who inspired the attack on the Mormon Salmon River mission, for he wanted the Indian country to be free of the whites. He soon became the recognized leader of an alliance consisting of the Shoshonean people of Oregon, Utah, and Nevada as well.[64]

The military authorities were aware of the growing threat of a general uprising in the Snake country, but were hampered by jurisdiction. Col. Albert Sidney Johnston, who had been sent to Salt Lake with his army in an anti-Mormon campaign, sent escorts of soldiers to accompany the wagon trains along the emigrant routes. On the Oregon Trail, his troops traveled as far west as Salmon Falls where they were relieved by patrols sent out from the Oregon District, who escorted the trains through the lower Snake country and into the Blue Mountains. Recognizing the awkwardness of the situation, he suggested that the military department of Utah be extended to the west and include the entire Snake River country of Washington Territory.[65]

In July 1860, several expeditions from Fort Dalles on the Columbia River were launched into the hostile country to the south and west. A squadron of dragoons from Fort Walla Walla was sent to "march along the Fort Boise or immigrant road . . . with the special purpose of guarding the road." After escorting what they believed to be the last wagon train through for the summer, they returned to their post after noting that the Idians were gathering in the mountains on both sides of the Snake River.[66] As soon as the troops departed, the Indians struck in a savage attack.

This incident was the "Otter Massacre" which occurred near Castle Rock on the alternate (southern) route of the Oregon Trail, south of old Fort Boise.[67] In one of the most desperate battles ever fought on the Snake River, a party of forty-four emigrants was besieged for two days before being forced to abandon their wagons and escape on foot. After a harrowing flight, fifteen survivors were eventually rescued. The blame for the attack was fixed on the Snakes of the Boise region.[68]

However, the hostile group crossed the Snake River onto the lower Weiser with four captive white children where they encountered Eagle-from-the-Light, a nontreaty Nez Perce chief whose band shared the high country with the Weiser Shoshoni. In a surprising move, the hostile chief and four "Snake Indians" departed immediately for Fort Walla Walla to report the guilty Indians to the authorities,[69] possibly to remove any suspicion from his own people and the Weiser Indians. The chief and his party were asked to go after the captives, but were later forced to turn back in their attempt due to the deep snow in the mountains.

The news that Eagle-from-the-Light (Tipyahlanah Kaupu) had been in the Weiser area must have caused apprehension for the whites: being one of the great leaders of the Nez Perce nation, he had not only opposed the Treaty of 1855, but had been urging war with the whites for years. In the spring of 1860, a party of miners had discovered gold on the Clearwater and prospectors were even then invading the Nez Perce heartland. The rush for gold would soon bring the whites into direct conflict with the Shoshoni peoples of southern Idaho.

THREE

The Miners and Settlers

THE SHOSHONI WAR

As a result of the Otter Massacre, the Office of Indian Affairs came under pressure to do something about the Indians in the Snake country. The Paiute bands south of the Columbia River, after years of being preyed upon by unscrupulous white immigrants, had united under Chief Winnemucca. The frontier was in flames, especially along the California route in northern Nevada.[1]

Making matters worse was the removal of the responsibility of Indian affairs for what is now western Idaho from Oregon to Washington Territory in 1861. Part of the problem was bureaucratic mess. Officially, in 1861, western Idaho *was* in Washington Territory. But in fact, for two years following statehood in 1859, Oregon still had the responsibility for Indian affairs in the western Idaho area. As late as 1862, the Washington superintendent, located far from the troubled region, appeared ignorant of the Shoshoni and their problems: "It is presumable that they are mostly within this Territory, as the sphere of their marauding operations commences south of Fort Hall, and extends to the Blue Mountains."[2]

The various military departments in Utah, Oregon, and Washington Territories were also under pressure to take action against the Snakes. Several expeditions were sent out in 1861, in an effort to recover the captive children of the Otter Massacre, but it was feared that they had perished in the mountains. According to some accounts, the identity of the band responsible for the attack was never learned.[3] Beginning in August 1861, the army was further hampered by reductions in troop strength, when the outbreak of the Civil War called for removal of troops to the East.

Eagle-from-the-Light had left his Shoshoni friends on the Weiser and returned to the Salmon River country. He found that hordes of miners had slipped south, across the Clearwater, to mine, in direct violation of an agreement made in April.[4] Eagle-from-the Light, disgusted over the new development and seeing that authorities would take no action, called a council at which he proposed to unite with the Shoshoni to drive out the white invaders. Red Owl (Koolkool Snehee), who had had a change of heart toward the whites, refused to go along and was supported by other noted headmen. In a huff, Eagle-from-the-Light "gathered together his lodges—abjured his nation forever as slaves to the whites, and took his departure for the Shoshones, with whom in the future he intend[ed] to cast his lot."[5]

The Sheepeaters on the Middle Fork of the Salmon were hidden away in their rugged mountain range, while the Weisers, to their west, remained isolated and relatively unknown to white officials.[6] The Weisers perceived no threat of a white invasion. The arrival of Eagle-from-the-Light and his band of hostile Nez Perce in the Weiser country probably heightened the war tempo initiated by Pasigo's Bannocks and the Boise Shoshoni.

In July 1862, a party of miners interrupted the Weisers' seclusion when they crossed the Salmon River and discovered gold in a basin on the northern edge of Weiser territory. Within a month, the report of the rich strike south of the Salmon reached thousands of prospectors and a stampede to Warren's Diggins (Warren) was under way. A simultaneous strike was made in the mountains southeast of the Weisers' homeland, when prospector George Grimes and his party of miners reached the Boise Basin. The Boise Indians attacked, killed Grimes, and drove the miners out, but the rush to the Boise Basin was on, and thousands of whites moved into the country.[7]

Worse yet, that same July, a wagon train led by early-day scout and pioneer Tim Goodale, crossed the Payette River seeking a route shorter than the Oregon Trail. Some of Goodale's party followed the Indian trail up the Weiser River and into the upper valley, where they got lost near the Weisers' winter camps. Failing to find a pass through the Seven Devils Mountains, they built a road over the mountains to the Brownlee Ferry below Hells Canyon.[8] Although the Weisers stayed clear of the white travelers and were relieved at their departure, the damage was done; the newly opened road through their territory was soon to become a major route to the new mines in Boise Basin.

It can only be speculated upon how the Weisers responded to white encroachment. Pasigo passed word to all the Snake groups that "when the leaves turn red" they would assemble; and: "When the leaves turn yellow and begin to fall," they would break into open warfare against the whites and destroy them.[9] The Weisers had ample opportunity to attack unsuspecting whites, but there is no indication that they did.

General Benjamin Alvord, commander of the U.S. Volunteers for the District of Oregon, was aware of the dangers of an outbreak of hostilities. He dispatched a force, under Lt. Col. Reuben F. Maury, to guard the Oregon Trail from Salmon Falls to west of Fort Boise and to punish or capture the Snake Indians responsible for the attack on the Otter train in 1860.[10] Able to hold some control over the hostile Indians by a show of force, the military authorities were powerless to stop or regulate the gold rush into the Indians' territory. General Alvord wrote from Fort Vancouver on October 15, 1862:

> Evil-disposed and abandoned white men may, as is rumored, have endeavored to incite them [Nez Perce] to revolt. . . . The Snakes may attack the outer mining camps south of Salmon River, but that must be expected. They are perpetually at war. Eagle from the Light, a Nez Perce chief who married a Snake woman, may have a small band of his people with him. It is rumored he is in affiliation with the Snakes.[11]

Though he was unable to control or stop the whites, General Alvord moved quickly to deal with the Indians. On October 24, 1862, he met the Nez Perce chiefs "in a grand council composed of Lawyer, Joseph, Big Thunder, and all the principal chiefs except Eagle of the Light [*sic*], who has never participated in any of the treaties."[12] Alvord and the Nez Perce agreed that the army would station troops on the Clearwater River to "protect the Indians" as the lawless country was being overrun with whiskey sellers and was "infested by robbers and cutthroats."

Unfortunately, military authorities failed to reach the Shoshoni to the south. In August 1862, Pasigo sent his long-awaited signal toward the east and the Shoshoni went to war. The Indians

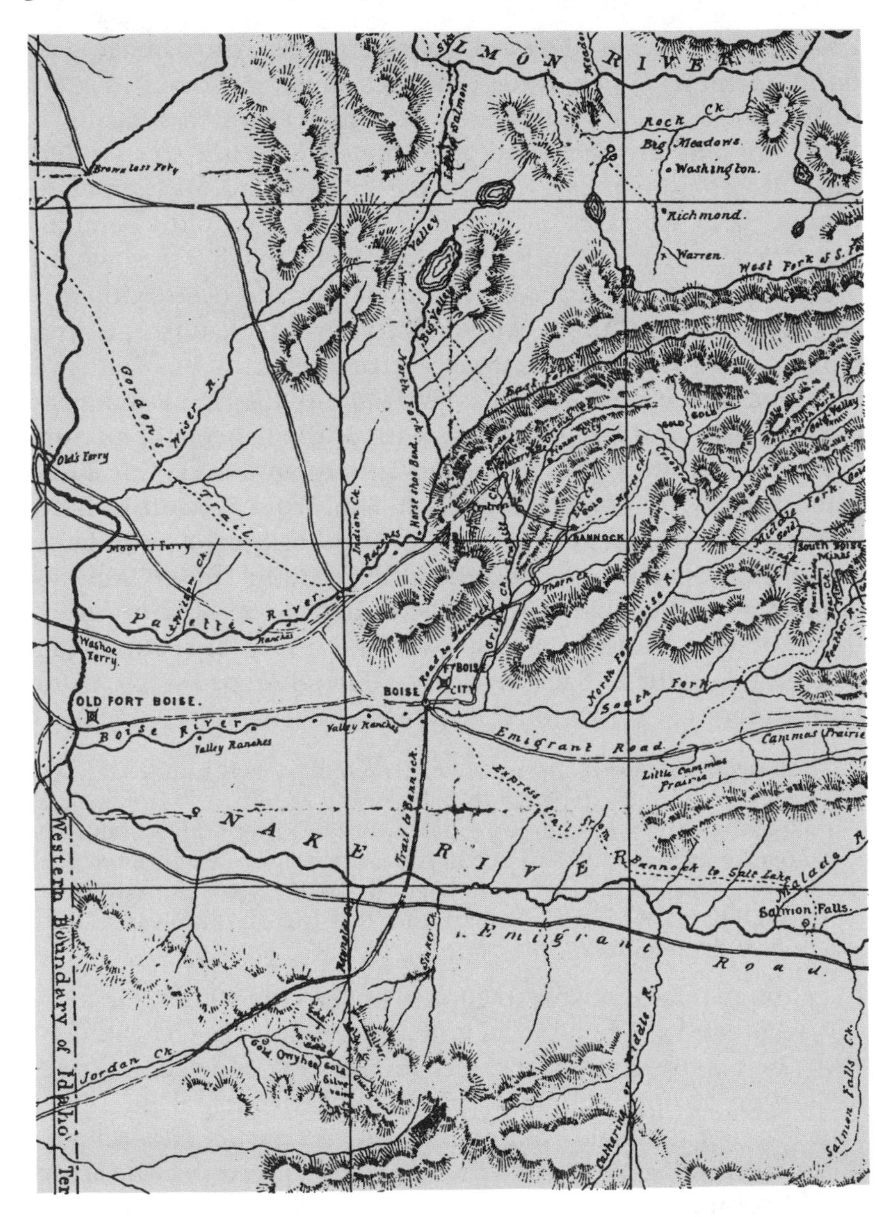

Section of George Woodman's "Map of the Mining Sections of Idaho & Oregon . . ." (1864). (Courtesy of The Bancroft Library)

lashed out in a series of attacks along the Oregon and California trails. Tales of murder and assault poured into white settlements on a daily basis. The situation in the eastern part of the territory was even more desperate; the ambush of several wagon trains by war parties from Pocatello's band near Massacre Rocks created great apprehension throughout the West.[13]

Colonel Patrick Connor and his California Volunteers arrived in Salt Lake City late in 1862. The approaching winter did not stop Connor from setting out to stop what he perceived as depredations by the Indians. On January 29, 1863, he found Bear Hunter's band in a winter camp on Bear River and, in a ruthless slaughter, massacred over two hundred people. At the end of the four-hour butchery, the army had lost 14 killed and 49 wounded while Indian losses were calculated at 224 killed and 160 women and children captured.[14]

The Battle of Bear River broke the spirit of the Northern Shoshoni and brought the war to a sudden, bloody, end.[15] It also fanned native opposition to the whites. As the hostile bands scattered into the safety of the mountains, news of the Bear River disaster spread throughout the Indian country. Word reached the Weisers at their isolated winter camps; unknown to them, white miners were preparing to invade their summer range that spring.

THE RUSH TO THE BASIN

The expected rush to Boise Basin in the fall of 1862 materialized, and the camps of Pioneer, Centerville, Placerville, Buena Vista, and Bannock City (later, Idaho City) were established. Thousands of miners, packers, gamblers, and merchants began to arrive, following the route which came in from the west. This main route was the old Indian trail "used by the Umatillas and other Indians of Oregon" to reach the council grounds on the Weiser River. Known to whites as the Brownlee Trail, it came down out of Oregon through the hills of the Grand Ronde Valley and crossed the Snake at the Brownlee Ferry, following the road blazed by the Goodale train the year before. After passing through the southern boundary of the Weiser country, it followed the Payette River as far as Horseshoe Bend before heading up Harris Creek into the Boise Basin.[16]

Another route, known as the Old Boise Trail, came from the north and passed through the Weisers' summer grounds. After reaching Salmon Meadows (later New Meadows), it crossed over into Long Valley and led south before going over Packer John Mountain onto the Middle Fork of the Payette River. After crossing the South Fork at Garden Valley, it climbed into the northern part of the basin.[17]

The newly arrived miners undertook to "do something" about the local Indians. They organized an expedition of eighty volunteers and, outfitted by local merchants, rode south under Captain Jeff Standifer on March 1, 1863. Scouring the Snake River Valley west and south into the Owyhee country, the expedition made indiscriminate attacks on any Indians in their path. After "dispatching reds" and taking several children prisoner, they returned to the basin.[18]

The military authorities were not idle during this time. The creation of Idaho Territory in March 1863 and the arrival of thousands of miners in the area called for the establishment of the long-proposed military fort on the Boise River and an expedition against the Snake Indians. On March 13, General Alvord wrote his superiors:

> The route thence to Boise would be through the country of Eagle of the Light [*sic*] over a pack trail. Eventually a wagon road may be found there. If I should not take this course, it will be because of the desire to get mounted troops to Boise before that date.[19]

Two commands that would threaten the peaceful existence of the Weisers were sent into the field. The first, under Major Pinckney Lugenbeel, arrived from the west to establish Fort Boise in the upper Boise Valley, near Table Rock.[20] A more immediate threat to the Weisers, however, was an expedition sent south from the Lapwai Agency. Three companies under Colonel Robert F. Maury, "whose object was to find and punish the Snakes,"[21] rode down the Salmon River and up the Old Boise Trail to the headwaters of the Payette and Weiser rivers. This expedition had no specific target; their purpose was to attack indiscriminately. The Weisers had evidently been warned of the approaching soldiers and had fled. A detachment under Captain George B. Currey rode south on the upper Weiser and found only a

Old Fort Boise, a Hudson's Bay trading post on the Snake River. (Courtesy of Idaho State Historical Society, neg. no. 1254-D)

deserted camp. Currey was convinced that "it had for years been the refuge of a band of Snakes which had plundered white travelers and settlers, successfully eluding pursuit or discovery."[22]

Unable to find the elusive Indians, Currey and his men headed toward the Boise River. These military men found the area "a pleasant country to travel through." One of the young lieutenants was so impressed with the Weiser area that he wrote a detailed description of the unexplored country that appeared in the *Oregon Argus* on July 27, 1863. The article created excitement for would-be settlers. Captain Currey reported that the valleys at the head of the Weiser and Payette rivers were "the most beautiful valleys in Idaho, the mountains that wall them in being covered with pine and tamarack trees, and the prairies verdant with nutritious grasses and clover."[23]

Maury's command arrived at the Boise River to find Major Lubengeel constructing the new post and civilians laying out plans for the townsite of Boise City. Within days Maury was resupplied and en route up the Snake toward Camas Prairie and the abandoned British post of Fort Hall in search of hostile bands of Shoshoni and Bannock. But, as in the Weiser area, there were

A group of Chief Pocatello's warriors. (Courtesy of National Anthropological Archives, Smithsonian Institution, neg. no. 1704-D)

no serious encounters and the command found only abandoned camps. A detachment of troops under Captain Currey did manage to overtake one small band of a dozen tipis, but "could not consent to fire upon an unarmed and supplicating foe." They took what stores of food they wanted as tribute and made the chief a prisoner. This was the end result of two hundred miles of hard traveling.[24]

Meanwhile, Colonel Connor and his California Volunteers were scouting southeastern Idaho. They met no resistance from the Shoshoni bands; the Shoshoni had lost their momentum to resist the whites and were forced to treat with the government.[25]

The Utah Superintendent of Indian Affairs, James D. Doty, signed a peace treaty with the Eastern Shoshoni, under Chief Washakie, in early July. Chief Pocatello sent word that the northwestern bands also wanted peace, and a treaty was signed at Box Elder on July 30, 1863.[26] Pasigo received word through Chief Winnemucca, of the Nevada Paiutes, to come for a conference with the whites. At a meeting on the Humboldt River, he had a "heap good talk" with John C. Burche of the Humboldt Agency and promised he would make no more attacks if the whites would also stop their aggressive acts.[27]

In 1863 five separate treaties were signed by Doty with various Shoshoni bands. It was unfortunate that the Boise Shoshoni and the bands of southwestern Idaho were excluded from the treaty process. This oversight resulted in more years of hardship and suffering for both whites and Indians.

The establishment of Fort Boise did much to curb the depredations of hostile bands in the area. With the creation of Idaho Territory and the appointment of the governor as Superintendent of Indian Affairs, the first clear policy regulating the responsibility for government relations was initiated.[28]

The problems with the Indians continued, especially in the newly discovered gold fields of the Owyhee Mountains. Two companies of volunteer miners in the Owyhee region took up arms in the summer of 1864 and engaged hunger-driven Indians in a pitched battle.[29] Minor depredations in the vicinity of Boise City reinforced white hostilities and put pressure on the authorities:

> Now what we want is more cavalry. Not for protection, but for chastisement of the Indians. We have had protection enough. It is now time that protection were made superfluous by at once removing the necessity for protection. We must either whip those Indians into peaceful behavior or kill them off.[30]

Governor Caleb Lyon moved to make peace. On October 10, 1864, he signed a treaty with the once powerful Boise Shoshoni and promised a reservation in return for the Boise Valley. The treaty was never ratified. Reaction by an Indian-hating public to the treaty attempt was expressed by a *Statesman* comment:

> No treaty with Snakes will have more force than a band of straw. Murder and plunder will be their future occupation. They admit they must steal or starve.

The skewed vision of the whites is evident in their descriptions of the Weiser and Payette area. During the initial white intrusion, one man wrote, "[T]he country was infested with several tribes of Indians."[31] The whites encamped near the areas of major Indian food sources, yet were frustrated when they encountered Indians on the trails and in the valleys. In fact, there was little danger from the Indians, "although they had plenty of chances to have killed defenseless people all along their route."[32]

White highwaymen and cattle thieves added another twist to the Indian problem in the Payette region. These outlaws often dressed as Indians, causing Paiute, Shoshoni, and Bannock to be blamed for many acts of which they were not guilty. Not all of the white settlers were taken in by such practices. William McConnell, a rancher who had settled in Jerusalem Valley above Horseshoe Bend, formed a vigilante committee in 1864. By the following year he had driven most of the outlaws from the Payette and Weiser valleys.[33]

THE SNAKE WAR OF 1866–68

By the middle of the 1860s, the Weiser band of Mountain Shoshoni, in reality still a kindred or group of related families, was under the direction of their headman and recognized leader, Eagle Eye. His name was English to begin with, not the translation of a Shoshoni term. His native name was, and still is today, pronounced [igrai]. Born sometime during the fur trade era, he helped influence those under his control to keep to their isolated mountain valleys and avoid contact with the whites. That a military expedition had entered their country searching for hostile Indians a few years earlier had reinforced his attitude. Even though the Weisers remained relatively unknown to the white world, they were in close contact with surrounding groups of Indians, and it is possible that Eagle Eye and his Weisers maintained a degree of control over other groups by suppressing hostile acts.[34]

The Boise Valley had been all but abandoned by visiting Shoshoni and other tribes of the Northwest as the great council grounds gave way to white expansionism and encroaching settlers. As for the Boise Shoshoni, their population and power had been decimated by war with the whites, and they had moved their village site to the protection of the military post. Native groups, those both hostile and friendly to whites, began to gather in the valleys of the upper Weiser River for their annual rendezvous.

To the south, Chief Egan (Ehegante, the Blanket-owner) led the roving Paiute groups who inhabited the country of the lower Weiser and Malheur along the Snake. Born a Shoshoni, but raised by Paiutes, he had strong family ties with Winnemucca's Paiutes of the Owyhee country and Nevada.[35] Although he was influenced by hostile bands of Paiutes in the south and west, he was also close friends with Eagle Eye and other members of the Weiser group and maintained peaceful relations with the whites while in the Weiser country. It wasn't long, however, until Egan had decided to cast his lot with the hostile groups and he and his Paiute followers were back on the Malheur River.

A smaller group of Shoshoni on the lower Weiser also remained friendly to the white people, as did a seemingly peaceful group under Yaggety, who lived along the lower Payette River.[36] Even the unpredictable Bannocks of the Payette, led by Bannock Joe, remained relatively friendly. The Nez Perce under Eagle-from-the-Light occasionally came down from the north, but they avoided conflicts though they displayed open contempt toward the whites.

Outside of the Weiser country, to the south and west, Eagle Eye had little or no control over the hostile actions of other groups. Problems in the Owyhee country escalated as gold-seeking whites poured into that fragile desert country. Although Pasigo and Winnemucca had sued for peace, other hostile leaders continued to terrorize the countryside. In an editorial on the state of affairs in March 1866, the *Idaho Statesman* reported that there were less than a "dozen peaceable, well-disposed

Indians, except the tribe of Sheep Eaters," who treated the whites "with kindness and cordiality."[37]

Howluck, "a considerable chief of the Snake Indians," whose associates ranged from the upper Weiser to central Oregon, encouraged the Klamath Lake, Modoc, and other Oregon bands to join in raids on the whites.[38] The Oregon bands under such chiefs as Wewawewa, Paulina, and Oytes escalated their attacks into open warfare, and by 1866, the frontier was once again in flames. The Oregon bands ranged throughout southern Oregon and the Owyhee country of southwestern Idaho and crossed the Snake to hit the newly developed ranches on the lower Weiser. In June the Buttermilk Ranch was hit by the "Malheur band of Snakes," and then escaped back across the Snake River. They fled to Burnt River, where they were "constantly committing depredations upon the Burnt River Valley."[39]

When troops failed to bring hostile Indians under control, white citizens placed bounties on them. The scalp of a "buck" was worth one hundred dollars, fifty dollars for a "squaw," and twenty-five for everything "in the shape of an Indian under ten." The hapless Boise and Bruneau Shoshoni, now peaceful, were at the mercy of white volunteers and scalp-hunting expeditions who saw every Indian as a threat. Agent Charles Powell speculated that these Shoshoni were indolent beings, motivated only when hungry, while the Bannock members, led by Bannock John, would "indulge the wild freedom they have hereto enjoyed" and were "given to martial displays, dancing, beating drums, etc."[40] Concerned for the Bannocks' safety, he moved them up to the forks of the Boise, thirty miles from the city, in July 1866.

Idaho's newly appointed territorial governor, D. W. Ballard, learned that the Boise, Bruneau, and Camas bands of Shoshoni were willing to go to a reservation. He recommended that a reservation be set aside for them.[41] The Department of the Interior instructed him to proceed, and the land for the Fort Hall Reservation was set aside in June of 1867.

During 1866 military authorities were pressured by whites to handle Indian problems. This pressure included scathing attacks by the press for military failure to force the Indians into submission. In an effort to crush the hostile bands operating south of the Snake River, the military department ordered General

George Crook to Fort Boise to assume command of the operations against the Snake Indians. Arriving on December 11, 1866, he found that affairs could not have been worse:

> That whole country, including Northern California and Nevada, Eastern Oregon and Idaho, up to Montana, you might say, was in a state of seige. Hostile Indians were all over the country, dealing death and destruction everywhere they wished. . . . There was scarcely a day that reports of Indian depredations were not coming in.[42]

Within a week of his arrival, reports of depredations near the mouth of the Boise River reached the post and Crook took to the field. He found that the hostiles had crossed the Snake and traveled up the Owyhee River. General Crook "got interested after the Indians" and did not return to Fort Boise for two years.[43] It was a stoke of luck for the Weisers that the military headed away from the Weiser area; because of this military diversion, they were able to escape disaster during the Snake War.[44]

With the army pursuing the hostile bands deep into their own territory, the Indians had little time to establish their winter camps or gather food. General Crook's strategy during the Snake campaign was to give the Indians no time to rest, regroup, or obtain supplies. To implement this relentless assault, he used winter expeditions and established temporary posts at strategic locations in hostile territory. The innovation of winter campaigns was later employed in other western regions.

Eagle Eye and the Weisers kept to the mountains during the fighting. Their existence was still unknown to the whites. Possibly, it was Eagle Eye's influence on the other native groups that encouraged them to avoid conflict in the Weiser area. If so, he was still powerless to stop Indian raids from across the Snake. By the spring of 1867, hostile groups were again committing depredations north of the river. In March, the ranches on the lower Weiser were again raided and hostile Indians made off with forty horses.[45]

General Crook's forces, meanwhile, chased the Indians deeper into Oregon. His methods were beginning to show results. There were pitched battles from the Owyhee country to the Steen's Mountain area. Small bands were either destroyed or they surrendered and were removed from the area. While the troops were effectively pursuing hostile Indians within Indian country, the whites of Idaho Territory had their own ideas on ridding the country of the Indian menace:

> This would be our plan of establishing friendship upon an eternal basis with our Indians: Let all the hostile bands of Idaho Territory be called in (they will not be caught in any other manner) to attend a grand treaty; plenty of blankets and nice little trinkets distributed among them; plenty of grub on hand; have a real jolly time with them; then just before the big feast put strychnine in their meat and poison to death the last mother's son of them.[46]

The military operations waged throughout the area against the Indians began to take its toll during 1867. In April a group of ranchers ambushed a war party led by Paulina in the John Day country. The powerful chief was killed. Fighting escalated during the summer, and the military continued their sortie into the winter months, as other bands were tracked down in the rugged desert country. Still, the Indians persisted in their offensive against the white invaders. In a strongly worded commentary, the editor of the *Idaho Statesman* reported that "almost every issue of this paper since its existence tells a story of some dark and bloody deed committed by Indians."[47]

War with the Indians made all bands open to suspicion and their intentions subject to question. Troubles on the lower Weiser had focused attention on the whole area. The whites were taken by surprise when a report reached Boise City, in June 1867, that a band of Indians were living near the head of the Weiser River and that this band "used every opportunity to make little raids" on the settlers in the valley. The Indians had been seen "lurking around the settlements. . . . Steak," reported the *Statesman*, "was doubtless the object." The *Statesman* promptly blamed the Weisers for grabbing an entire train a few weeks earlier.[48]

The Weiser River Shoshoni had finally been discovered by the whites. Though, under normal policy, the military would have immediately sent a scouting party to the Weiser area, they were unable to in this case. The troops were busy fighting the Snake War to the west. Three months later, in September 1867, Eagle Eye's people were declared to be hostiles. Reports had once again come in of depredations on the lower Weiser. This time the army responded with troops. Their orders were to "proceed to the Weiser river, and destroy the band of hostile Indians now marauding on said river and in its vicinity."[49]

Lieutenant Thomas Barker, "an experienced Indian fighter," set out on October 4, and headed into the Weiser area. The Weisers, finding themselves hunted by a military expedition, stayed one step ahead of the advancing troops and retreated east, into the rugged Salmon River country. Barker discovered that the supposed depredations on the Weiser River had been committed not by the local Weisers, but by Indians who had crossed over to the Weiser from the Snake for the purpose of hunting. The Indians had crossed back and had headed in the direction of Farewell Bend and, contrary to reports, no depredations had taken place.

Scouting the country, Barker found Eagle Eye's abandoned camp and concluded that it had been occupied by seventy-five to eighty Indians. In the deserted camp, Barker found footprints measuring seventeen and one-half inches. The press immediately took note of this report, and the *Idaho Statesman* offered "fifty dollars for the big toe of this babe of the woods, and his topknot would readily command one hundred in coin."[50]

The legend of "Bigfoot" was launched overnight, and the phantom's tracks were reported all over the countryside. It was said the Weisers themselves helped spread the legend by using huge stuffed moccasins to make the menacing footprints.[51] Whether they intended to terrorize the local settlers and troops, perpetrate the story as a joke, or use big moccasins for foot protection is not known, but the effect was the same. With the real Bigfoot, a hostile Indian leader named Howluck, at large in the Owyhee country, the legend of a shadowy and terrifying character (perpetrated by wild reports and an imaginative press) spread throughout the Northwest.

Not all whites had classified the Weiser Indians as a hostile group associated with the Snake War. The Weisers' retreat into Salmon River country was noted by miners who reported their location on the South Fork of the Salmon. Governor David W. Ballard wrote to the Commissioner of Indian Affairs that "towards the centre of the territory, in the neighborhood of 'Warrens,' is a small band of about 100 friendly Shoshones." He urged that the Fort Hall Reservation, established in June but still unoccupied, be used to locate the friendly Indians of southern and central Idaho in order to isolate them from the "wild, vicious, wandering and warlike people" who were attacking whites.[52]

Ballard met with the brothers, Bannock John and Bannock Jim (Pagwite), headmen of the Boise, Camas, and Bruneau bands of Shoshoni and Bannocks, several months earlier on the Boise River, but the leaders refused to speak for any of the tribes because of the absence of Taghee (one of various spellings), their recognized chief. On August 21, 1867, Taghee was present when the Indians called the governor to an informal council of their own. They listened to Ballard's argument for removing them to the new reservation and giving up claim to their country. The frustrated Taghee responded:

> I thought when the white people came to Soda Springs and built houses and put soldiers in them, it was to protect my people, but now they are all gone, and I do not know where to go nor what to do.
>
> The white people have come into my country, and have not asked my consent. Why is this? I have never known what the white people wanted me to do. I have never killed white people who were passing into my country. What you say to me I shall never forget. All the Bannock Indians will obey me and be good, but the Sheep-eaters are not my people . . . I will answer for the Bannocks. The Boise and Bruneaus are poor; they cannot travel far; they have no horses to hunt buffalo, but they are good Indians, and are my friends. . . .[53]

In the formal agreement that followed, it was written that the Indians would move to the reservation the following spring, but this did not happen.

Agent Luther Mann of Fort Bridger identified the Sheepeaters as a secretive band who lived in the Salmon River Mountains, and Utah Superintendent of Indian Affairs, F. H. Head, concluded that the Sheepeaters fell under the provisions of the Treaty of Soda Springs of 1863. Even though Taghee had refused to speak for the Sheepeaters, Governor Ballard recognized the necessity of coming to terms with these Mountain Shoshoni. As part of his agreement with Taghee's people, Bannock John consented to influence what Sheepeaters he could to abide by the terms.[54]

But the enterprising headman Eagle Eye refused to subject his Weiser kinsmen to starvation on the upper Boise, where they would be preyed upon by unscrupulous whites. The Snake War had escalated, and it was a risk for Indians, friendly or otherwise, to be searching for food in the lower country.[55] Always alert, Eagle Eye and his people spent the winter of 1867 unmolested in the mountains.

In May 1868, the Indian Peace Commission sent General C. C. Augur to Fort Bridger to negotiate with the "Snakes, Bannocks, and other Indians." Augur was met by the Bannocks under Taghee and Chief Washakie and his Eastern Shoshoni. In the treaty council that followed, it was established that the new Fort Hall Reservation would be opened for the settlement of the Bannocks when Taghee insisted that he would not go to a reservation in the Wind River country, but wanted "the Porte Neuf country and Kamas plains."[56]

When the eastern groups of Sheepeaters, who had chosen to live with the Lemhi Sheepeaters under Tendoy (Un-ten-doip, he likes broth), learned that Taghee and the Bannocks had received $4,000 worth of treaty goods, a group led by Captain Jim, son of the former Boise Shoshoni leader Peiem, arrived in Boise City in July to take issue with Governor Ballard over the inequity. Word came from Montana that Tendoy's people were living in "misery, filth, and dire want," and Agent Mann was sent to investigate the situation. Agent Mann verified the accounts.[57] On September 24, 1868, a treaty was concluded with Tendoy and his followers at Virginia City, Montana. The Indians agreed to cede all their claims to lands outside a small reservation in the Lemhi Valley, but the U.S. Senate failed to ratify the treaty.

The Boise, Camas, and Bruneau Indians, like Tendoy's Sheepeaters, were also upset over the treaty presents to the Bannocks. They failed to understand why Taghee had received goods and they had been left out. Indian anger and envy created by the affair led the *Boise Democrat* to warn, "We do not want any child's play in regard to Indian Affairs."[58] Seeing trouble on the horizon, Governor Ballard and Agent Charles Powell hurried to set up the Fort Hall Reservation for the immediate removal of the Indians. Powell, without regard to political considerations, had his own reasons for wanting the Indians removed to the reservation. He reported:

> The peculiar situation of the Indians under my charge has compelled me to confine them to certain narrow and circumscribed limits. On the one hand were the hostile Snakes and Piutes, on the other the whites, who for the most part entertain a deadly hostility towards all Indians, and who had settled on most of the valley lands, besides being scattered over the mountains in quest of the various metals.
>
> The more ignorant and unscrupulous look on the Indian as a common bird of prey, to be plucked and destroyed at will, and I regret to add that even the more intelligent and better class lend them aid and countenance in that direction, subjecting these Indians to difficulties, annoyances, and even death.[59]

The Snake War was coming to its inevitable conclusion during these treaty efforts by the civilian authorities. In May 1868, troops captured Chief Egan and ten lodges of his Paiutes on the North Fork of the Malheur River near Castle Rock. The following month, Howluck and sixty-one of his band were taken by surprise in eastern Oregon. The Winnemuccas, a Paiute band under Chief Winnemucca, were captured soon afterward and sent to Fort Smith, thus forcing Wewawewa and the other hostile leaders to sue for peace. Meeting with Crook at Fort Harney in July, the Indians, run into the ground by Crook's vigorous winter campaign, surrendered. The general told them that if they remained peaceful and surrendered stolen property, they could go free. He had difficulty with whites who had no faith in Indians promises, but even those whites eventually realized the need to remove obstacles to peace. The press declared the Snake War officially over.[60]

FOUR

A Time of Troubles

THE FIRST ATTEMPTS AT REMOVAL

With the restoration of peace following the Snake War, a sense of normalcy was restored to the whites. The military authorities returned to their posts and resumed their duties, while patrols were sent out after the scattered bands that continued to resist. By August 1868, most operations had ceased and the conflict had been brought to an end.[1]

Governor Ballard and his agents were still planning for the removal of the Boise and Bruneau Shoshoni who had no treaty with Washington. Because there was no money, the bands were now destitute and were to be given priority in the movement to Fort Hall. Governor Ballard made repeated requests to Washington for funds to take care of the nearly six hundred Shoshoni still on the upper Boise.[2]

Eagle Eye and his Weiser Shoshoni had spent the winter of 1867–1868 out of reach of the white troops while the Snake War was brought to its conclusion. When word of peace reached them, they felt safe enough to return to their valley on the upper Weiser River, even though their territory to the west was being overrun by miners: gold had been discovered on the Gold Fork diggings of the Payette River. Miners were not only moving into the upper Payette, but were also exploring the South Fork of the Salmon. A strike at Leesburg, on the east side of the Salmon River Mountains, was focusing attention on the unexplored heartland of the independent Sheepeater families in the Middle Fork country.[3]

The reports from the Weiser area in 1868 indicating that Indians were seen "lurking about" were not unfounded. The Weisers, trying to maintain their shy existence, had found white settlers moving into their upper valleys. The rich soil, streams lined with cottonwood, and mountains forested with pine and fir created too tempting a site to be passed up by settlers. In early 1868 the first permanent white settlers departed from the Lower Weiser into the mountains to the north. They passed through the uninhabited Middle Valley into what was then known as the Upper Weiser Valley to homestead.[4]

Before long news reached the authorities at Boise that the elusive "band of thieving Snakes" was once again on the headwaters of the Weiser. An experienced scouting party was led by Colonel James B. Sinclair dispatched by the commander of Fort Boise on July 16, 1868. The small expedition was composed of the colonel, nine enlisted men, the well-known chief of scouts, Sinora Hicks, and seven Boise Shoshoni scouts. Traveling light and fast, the command packed only eight days rations and headed for the upper Weiser.[5]

Eagle Eye and the other Weiser headmen learned of this threat and once again abandoned their camp. But this time, Colonel Sinclair was determined to bring the elusive Indians to terms. He followed the trail of the main group over the mountains and overtook them near the junction of the Little Salmon River and the Salmon River. Forty-one people were taken prisoner, including Eagle Eye and twelve of his men and twenty-eight women and children. Eagle Eye and his followers had twenty-one horses with them, as well as a large quantity of dried salmon and camas roots.[6]

There was no evidence of emigrant plunder among the Weisers' belongings. One thing Sinclair's men did find, however—and which looked suspicious—was a pair of moccasins over sixteen inches long, stuffed with rags and fur, that "could be used to make a fearful looking track . . . which a man with a little bad whiskey in him would swear was made by an Indian seventeen feet high."[7]

The colonel suspected that other members of Eagle Eye's group were still in the vicinity, and he spent thirteen days searching the countryside before he was convinced there were no more Weisers in the area. Living off the meager food supply he had taken from the Indians, Colonel Sinclair returned to Fort Boise with his captives. The first reports released to the public established that the captives were not the Snake Indians who had been committing depredations, but were, instead, a group of Boise Indians that had become separated from the others and were afraid to return.

The *Idaho Statesman* noted that Colonel Sinclair's expedition cleared up the Indian question in that part of the territory and had created friendly relations between the Weiser Indians and the whites which would last until the Indians could be removed to Fort Hall.[8]

Within a few days, Eagle Eye met with Governor Ballard and the army commanders. He was questioned about his people and their attitude toward whites. Ballard was to decide what to do with the Weisers: send them to Wewawewa at Steen's Mountain; turn them over to the agent in charge of the Boise and Bruneau Indians; or let them return to their hunting and fishing grounds on the Weiser.[9] After the meeting, he decided to release them, and they immediately returned to the mountains.

Several weeks later depredations were reported on the Weiser. Special Agent George Hough left Boise on September 7, 1868, to check on Eagle Eye and his group. The *Statesman*, in one of its mildest attacks on the Indians, offered only that "if they are the band lately captured they should be placed in a locality where they cannot do any harm in the future."[10] It was one of the first times since the paper had been in existence that it did not cry for blood or revenge.

The Weiser families settled at their old winter camp on the Little Weiser River, named Indian Valley by the whites. The valley opened into the northern end of the upper Weiser Valley, where a half dozen families of settlers lived. Though it is probable that feelings of mistrust and suspicion existed between the whites and the Weisers, there was also evidence of accommodation. Eagle Eye and the other headmen recognized the inevitable. The whites were there to stay and, for their own good, the Weisers would have to accept the situation. Through their friends and from the Boise Shoshoni, being herded like cattle on the upper Boise, they had learned what resistance to change could mean. They also learned through the Boise Indians, to their dismay, that the white authorities had plans of removing them to Fort Hall.[11]

Indian Valley. (Photo by author)

Sonora Hicks, the former chief scout out of Fort Boise, and a private citizen named Walter Mason spent the winter hunting and prospecting in the mountains during 1868–1869 and decided to visit the Weisers' camp. Eagle Eye and his companions received them cordially, in spite of the fact that the scout had been one of those responsible for their capture a few months earlier.

The two men spent several months in the vicinity. They learned much about the Indian group, and it can be assumed that the Indians learned just as much about the whites. During this time, the Weisers told Hicks and Mason that another unknown group of Indians lived on the other side of the mountains about twenty miles away and shared in the fishing in the valley. These "wild Indians," the white men later reported, were hostile toward whites and had "never before seen a white man except to take a scalp." While the two white men were there, Eagle Eye sent two of his men to their camp, inviting them to a council. Twenty-nine came into the Weiser camp for a visit with the whites. They sat in silence for over two hours smoking a peace pipe, until the white men could no longer stand it and opened a dialogue. They were surprised to find the Indians wanted to converse, and a "big talk" followed where the Indians told them that they wanted to talk to the "Big Captain" of the whites.[12]

Eagle Eye let Hicks know that he and his people were friendly, but had fears that the "wild Indians might commit some depredations for which he would be held responsible by the whites." A council was held the evening before Hicks and Mason left the valley. The Weisers said they wanted to be friends with the whites, but they also told them they had no intention of going to the reservation at Fort Hall. Eagle Eye told the two that there was no objection to sharing their valley with the whites, so long as whites did not interfere with the Indians' fishing privileges. The Weisers emphasized that, if left where they were, they could supply themselves with the food they needed without any assistance from the government.[13]

Upon their return to Boise in February 1869, Mason reported that the Weiser band, about seventy in number, was well supplied with horses and firearms and that if they were taken to Fort Hall they would only be "retained with great difficulty."[14] Eagle Eye, Mason said, had no intentions of taking his people out of their beloved valley and subjecting them to the same conditions the Boise Indians were enduring. Awaiting removal to Fort Hall, the Boise and Bruneau bands were starving. By December, no funds had arrived to help them through the winter months, and they had scattered over the countryside searching for food.[15] Some had taken to begging in the streets of Boise or doing odd jobs around the city, some lost their blankets in bets to white men who induced them into running footraces. Worse, an epidemic of measles, a sickness that could be deadly to Indians, had hit the Indian camp above Boise.

Governor Ballard decided to use what money was available to move the Boise Shoshoni to Fort Hall as soon as spring came. He sent Agent Charles F. Powell to set up the reservation and to see what other Indians could be induced to settle there.[16] Most of the Boise and Bruneau Shoshoni accepted the situation, but a few were reluctant to leave their old homeland. Even some of the whites were saddened by the prospect, prompting the editor of the *Statesman* to mention that they were not really bad Indians and that their departure would add some inconvenience for the whites. As a parting shot, he added, "The town looks better, however, without them than with them strolling about in their uncouth garb, or no garb at all, as the case may be."[17]

The exodus of the Indians took place on March 13, 1869: 1,150 Boise and Bruneau Shoshoni and 150 Bannocks were escorted by soldiers to the Fort Hall Reservation, gathering scattered groups along the Snake River en route. The Sheepeaters beyond Wood River and Eagle Eye's group on the upper Weiser refused to move.[18]

Walter Mason's visit and his attempt to urge Eagle Eye to go to Fort Hall had been met, understandably, by an adamant people who stubbornly refused to give up their independence and become wards of the government. One hundred and fifty Weisers had been identified by whites. They ranged from fifteen miles above the mouth of the Weiser to the Salmon River. They were described by whites as "quite friendly and take as much interest in suppressing hostile bands as can be expected of them," and the newly arrived settlers, who recognized the value of having the protection of the Weiser Indians, did not want the group removed.[19]

As the push to remove all Indians to reservations gained momentum across Idaho Territory in the 1860s, many submitted voluntarily. Pocatello's Northwestern Shoshoni and Taghee's Bannocks arrived at Fort Hall in June and were anxious to settle there permanently. Tendoy's Lemhis, like the Weisers, refused to give up their valley for the Fort Hall Reservation and preferred to starve in Montana, where they were reportedly living on gophers.[20]

More and more of the independent families of Sheepeaters from central Idaho joined the Lemhi and Weiser Shoshoni. The gold strike at Leesburg had brought thousands of white miners into Sheepeater territory, and though most of the miners were gone now, the strike at Loon Creek brought more. The Shoshoni could not maintain their life-style in a country overrun by whites. Those who could obtain horses or wanted the Plains life-style came down out of the mountains to join the Lemhi on the Salmon River to the east. Many of the loose village groups, such as the

Sheepeater Indians encamped on Medicine Lodge Creek and photographed by William H. Jackson in 1871. (Courtesy of National Anthropological Archives, Smithsonian Institution, neg. no. 1713)

Pasasigwana Sheepeaters, who were north of Camas Prairie on the Salmon River, moved as a unit to the Lemhi Valley.[21]

Others of these loose groups, who lacked horses or preferred more traditional ways, traveled west to join the Weiser group under Eagle Eye. Andy Johnson, headman of a Sheepeater group on the South Fork of the Salmon, had a Weiser wife, and his people eventually became permanent members of the Weiser band. The Sheepeaters of the Middle Fork had a nearly identical life-style too, and were in closer contact with, the Weisers, with whom they often fished and hunted, than with their Lemhi relatives under Tendoy. One source noted "68 Weiser Shoshones" in 1869, even though other sources the same year indicated over one hundred and fifty were in the group.[22] The independent status of its members, who often preferred to hunt and fish as individuals or as family groups in the summer months, made an accurate census difficult. It is generally believed that they rarely exceeded a hundred in a village at any one time. A possible exception to this was when they were visited by wandering groups of Paiutes, Bannocks, or Nez Perces, who often took up temporary residence with Eagle Eye's Weiser people.

Going into the 1870s, it was clear that the native population respected the Weisers. Eagle Eye kept his word to the white authorities and there were no more acts of violence in the Weiser country, despite the presence of hostile bands who again began frequenting the area following the end of the Snake War. During this period, the Weiser Shoshoni were developing both socially and politically toward a loosely organized, restricted form of "band" organization. They were well armed and possessed many horses, but their size made them less of a threat than the larger, predatory bands who came into the valley when the annual rendezvous was resumed. It was probably Eagle Eye's leadership ability and oratory skill which persuaded these groups to keep the upper Weiser a place of peace.

In the summer of 1869, the first whites settled on the Little Weiser River (Indian Valley), which was the site of the Weisers' winter camps. In the aftermath of the gold rush in southern Idaho, the Payette and the Weiser valleys were attracting whites who came to stay and build permanent homes. They constructed houses, stables, and barns; grubbed out sagebrush and fenced fields.[23] The Indians did not oppose their arrival; they probably viewed the whites more with curiosity than resentment. Council Valley, ten miles to the north of Indian Valley and site of an annual rendezvous, however, remained uninhabited by the whites.

Regardless of Eagle Eye's willingness for peace or the desires of the local whites who wanted them to stay, the authorities were intent on removing the Weiser Shoshoni to Fort Hall. The agents and their emissaries had tried, unsuccessfully, to lure the Weisers away from their valley, and their failure was becoming a source of frustration for the government. Governor Ballard reported to the Commissioner of Indian Affairs in 1869, that there were still some "renegade" Bannocks, Sheepeaters, and Boise Indians who would not go to the reservation "until some of them are killed."[24]

Before Governor Ballard could act, the Commissioner of Indian Affairs took away the responsibility of superintendent from the governor's office and initiated the practice of appointing military officers within the agency. Colonel De Lancey Floyd-Jones arrived in Boise on June 12, 1869, and was followed in July by Lieutenant W. H. Danilson, who replaced Powell at Fort Hall.[25]

After conferring with Governor Ballard and the authorities at the Fort, Colonel Floyd-Jones made the removal of the Weiser people one of his first priorities. In mid-August, he set out with Colonel Sinclair and a small military detachment to visit Eagle Eye's camp on the Weiser, to "ascertain the exact number and condition of the small band with a view of transferring them to Fort Hall."[26] The new superintendent reported that it was unrealistic to expect the Indians to give up their freedom and lifestyles to immediately adopt the "domestic habits of the white man."[27]

Sinclair's visit to Fort Hall the following month had a sobering effect, and the plan to remove the Weisers was delayed. The farming effort at Fort Hall had failed. There were 1,100 Indians living there and only thirty-five acres had been planted. Seven acres had produced some potatoes and turnips, but the grasshoppers and drouth had destroyed the grainfields.[28] Washington was not sending enough funds for those Shoshoni and Bannocks that continued to come onto the reservation. Lack of funds would plague the Fort Hall Reservation and its agents for years to come.

THE EARLY 1870S

While many Indians came into the upper country simply to trade, rest, and pasture their horses before moving on, the Weiser Indian population had established three permanent winter camps in Indian Valley. Two of these camps represented some of the Nez Perce under a peaceful headman known to the whites as Indian Charley, who had chosen to settle with the Weiser Shoshoni. Another man of importance within the native population was the Sheepeater leader, Andy Johnson, identified as both a brother and brother-in-law of Eagle Eye, though the latter designation is probably correct.[29] Just when Bear Skin and his few Bannocks joined the group is not known. Big John, Captain John and Chuck (a Lemhi), all had degrees of influence within the little society, but all of these men recognized Eagle Eye as "Hyas Tyhee," or leader. Still, though the groups of Indians were easily recognizable in their own day, it should be noted here, they were destined to never be classified as a true band in the classical sense, or qualify as a unitary political entity by modern anthropologists and the term "band" in this work is strictly used as a historical concept.

The Weisers were an easily identifiable people when compared to other Shoshoni who frequented the area. The influence of the cultural elements contributed by the Nez Perce and Bannock members left a visible mark on the Sheepeater group. Their Paiute neighbors and the many Indian visitors to the area also brought in certain traits that were probably absorbed by the members. By the 1870s, the Weisers were easily recognized by the whites as a distinct group and were referred to, in laymen terms, as a "mixed band," thereby resulting in a great deal of controversy over their original identity and sociopolitical organization by later historians.

Eagle Eye kept the visiting Indians quiet in 1870, in spite of the fact that tribes from throughout the Northwest were returning in larger numbers than before to the rendezvous in Indian and Council valleys. White authorities, hard pressed to take care of the problems plaguing the Fort Hall Reservation, were content to let the Weisers take care of themselves; Superintendent Floyd-Jones and Agent Danilson could not keep the Shoshoni they were already responsible for on the reservation. The Indians, the *Statesman* reported, kept drifting away to dig roots at Camas Prairie, or to head back toward the Boise River, much to the alarm of the local whites. With rations nearly exhausted and no funds forthcoming, Danilson reported that "the Agency is destitute of nearly all kinds of winter supplies."[30]

Before the two military men could get control of the situation, another shake-up in the Indian service took place. In July 1879 Congress passed legislation that excluded the practice of appointing military men to the reservations. Indian welfare was turned over the churchmen of various faiths, and "the agencies were shuffled among the churches like so many decks of cards."[31]

A typical Shoshoni village in the mountains. (Courtesy of National Anthropological Archives, Smithsonian Institution, neg. no. 1668)

The bewildered Indians at the Fort Hall and Lemhi agencies were to find yet other new agents, under the direction of the Methodist Episcopal church. In December, Agent Danilson was replaced by newly appointed J. H. High at the Fort Hall Reservation, but High's tenure was short-lived. The reservation was reassigned to the Roman Catholic church several months later, and Montgomery P. Berry was named as agent in March 1871.[32] During this tumultuous time, the Idaho superintendency was dissolved and the agents were ordered to report directly to the Commissioner of Indian Affairs in Washington.

If Eagle Eye and his band had hopes of making an agreement, or gaining a small reserve in the Weiser Valley, as Tendoy had obtained for his people in the Lemhi, these constant shifts of affairs and personnel discouraged them. Adding insult to injury, the Congress, in March 1871, passed an act declaring that the United States no longer recognized the Indian tribes as sovereign nations and that tribes henceforth would be dealt with through executive orders and not treaties.[33]

The problems at Fort Hall had a direct effect on the Weiser Indians who were finding relations with the whites precarious. During Agent High's short tenure at Fort Hall, the Indians left the reservation in large groups to search for food. The arrival in Boise Valley in June of a large contingent of Shoshoni, led by headman Captain Jim, or Jim Collins as he was now being called, had caused a stir. Most of the Indians had pitched their tipis at Middleton and a few were at Government Island, below Boise. Others had camped at Warm Springs and near the penitentiary above the town. After visiting the Fort and informing the military authorities of their peaceful intentions, Collins, Little Jim, and several Bannock chiefs rode down to the city to meet with Secretary E. J. Curtis, acting governor, and other officials. Curtis flatly informed the Indians they were not welcome in Boise Valley. In a dramatic speech to the assembled authorities, Collins unleashed his own feelings on the whites:

> Governor, all my people come here for peace and pleasure. Collins was born in this valley, long and many snows, long 'fore white man he come here. In rocks by warm springs here, Collins bury his father and mother. I come here, I, Collins, all years to these graves. These braves all the same as me. They have ol' people, all buried same as Collins, and all sleep in this valley. We know we be Injuns but we have dead people and we like our dead people . . . I sorry no white man like it. I say good-by. I go home now, Fort Hall. Next twelve moon, when grass he grows good, all come 'gain to see our dead. Not you, not Great Father, can stop us, not soldiers can!"[34]

Their return to western Idaho was noticed by the press, who complained that the "red devils" seemed to understand military troops at Fort Boise had been reduced. Large bands were reportedly annoying the settlers with presumptuous demands for "grub, tobacco, whisky, and other property, and by conduct that may be best described as general cussedness. . . . Their behavior on Payette, Weiser, Squaw Creek, Willow Creek, and in Camas Prairie, comes under the head of that general cussedness with which the troubles are inaugurated." The *Statesman* suggested that if the whites had to defend themselves, a war of extermination might be the answer.[35]

The presence of the reservation Indians gave the press exciting news for a time, though accounts were often exaggerated concerning events in southwest Idaho. The truth was, even though many small Shoshoni bands had quietly left the reservation to hunt and fish, "they molested neither white men nor their crops."[36] After Chief Taghee died early in 1871, the Bannocks were fragmented and disorganized. Most were in buffalo country, to the relief of Agent High, who did not have enough food to keep them at the reservation.[37]

In 1871 only eighty-three Weisers were permanently located in Indian Valley.[38] They played host to many visiting Indians, sharing their pastures and valley with the bands, and showed a remarkable degree of influence in controlling so many Indians camped in such close proximity to white settlers. Despite Eagle Eye's apparent restraining influence, insecure white settlers were apprehensive. The presence of known hostiles in the area heightened the situation.

In July a report from Horseshoe Bend said that two men had been killed and fifty head of stock had been run off on the Malheur River. Eagle-from-the-Light and his Nez Perce band were blamed for the attack because they were known to be "prowling 'round in that vicinity. . . . Their head-quarters have been on the Weiser, Little Salmon and Snake river, below the big bend, and have been on the rob and kill in a small, stealthy way for the last ten years." Whether the accounts were true or not, the editor of the *Statesman* continued, Eagle-from-the-Light and the Nez Perce formed the nucleus for other bad Indians and, he added, they should be "brought under subjection" or, if not, "exterminated." The problem, he concluded, was "permitting the Indians to wander away from the reservations."[39]

An appeal to the military from government officials and private citizens for troops to keep the Indians on the reservations was denied. General Edward Canby pointed out that one of the major problems stemmed from the use of Camas Prairie by white settlers. Though the Camas Prairie was part of the lands claimed for the reservation, the Shoshoni had been content to share it with the whites, who pastured their stock there. They were "outraged" to find, however, that a herd of hogs was destroying the camas fields.[40]

As a tegwani (talker), Eagle Eye had only limited influence over the behavior of Indians who visited the Weiser Valley during the month of July. The whites were relieved when the last group of them left and no serious confrontations had taken place. By September, the Weisers and the settlers in the upper valleys were preparing for winter. At Fort Hall that month, Agent Berry was forced to send the Shoshoni off the reservation again to hunt.[41]

The Weisers were adapting to the presence of white settlers in their valley and, by 1872, the two races were becoming more friendly. Many of the settlers recognized that it was the presence of Eagle Eye and the Weisers who formed a sphere of protection for them. Described as "peace-loving and helpful," a few of the Weisers had taken up the habit of helping white families with the harvest of grass hay.[42]

With the coming of the July rendezvous, tensions again began to mount, however. In a lengthy editorial, the *Statesman* discussed some of the legal and political considerations of retaining Indians on the reservations or at Camas Prairie. The editorial erroneously stated that Camas Prairie was "common ground" for both whites and Indians. The editor also declared that the Indians had no right to travel through the country or "congregate on the Weiser, or in any other settlements." He further noted that there were now two white settlements on the Weiser, "known as the Upper and Lower Weiser settlements" with "about seventy-five souls in each"[43]

Fort Hall had an improved harvest in 1872, but it was not sufficient to sustain the resident Indians, and Agent Berry allowed them to leave. He was immediately placed on the defensive again for his actions. He explained to his superiors that, under the treaty rights, the Indians had the right to hunt on unoccupied lands and a legal right to Camas Prairie. He also pointed out that hostilities would arise if there were whites at Camas Prairie who fed their hogs on the camas crop.[44]

Adding to the tensions over the situation at Fort Hall and to those elicited by the rendezvous, it was learned that "600 Umatilla Indians at La Grand, Oregon," were on their way to the Weiser to meet the Shoshoni and Bannocks. The Indians were expected to number over two thousand. "The principal object of this meeting is to have horse races, swap horses, trade squaws, gamble, and have a big pow-wow generally." The real fear, the

Governor Thomas Bennett. (Courtesy of Idaho State Historical Society)

Statesman pointed out, was not of friendly Indians, but that ''all the bad Indians follow these expeditions'' and assemble on the outskirts of defenseless settlements, who are ''at the mercy of these barbarous savages.'' Blame was fixed on the agents for allowing the ''marauding bands'' to leave the reservations in the first place.[45]

Idaho Territorial governors had a turnover rate greater than that of the Indian agents. When newly arrived Governor Thomas Bennett learned that the reservation Indians had left Camas Prairie and were heading to the Weiser country with "bad Bannocks following along," he set out with Major Downey (no first name is mentioned in the records) and intercepted them at Willow Creek, forty-five miles east of the capital. Not only were the Fort Hall Indians led by Bannock Jim there, but Tendoy and his Lemhi band were with them. Meeting the Indian leaders for a "talk," it was learned that the Indians were "scared" and had no intention of going to war, but only wanted to visit their friends on the Weiser. After informing the Indians that they must not go there, Bennett extracted a promise that they would return to Camas Prairie and, satisfied that he had accomplished his mission, he reported that "there will be no further trouble and the Indians will go back as they promised."[46]

When these Indians from Camas Prairie learned that the Umatillas had reached the upper Weiser and were afraid to travel on to Camas Prairie because of possible trouble with the whites, they continued west to the rendezvous on the Weiser River. An embarrassed Governor Bennett was powerless to take action, and the *Statesman* continued to print blazing editorials on the "Indian threat." In Silver City, however, the *Owyhee Avalanche* reported the Indians were peaceful and accused the Boise editor of exaggerating the reports.[47]

The congregation of Indians on the Weiser, during July and August of 1872, was one of the largest yet in the upper country. Eight hundred Umatillas (Cayuses) were joined by 500 Nez Perces, 75 Klikitats, and 1,125 Shoshoni and Bannocks, making a total of about 2,500 at the encampment. The presence of a white man named Bane, sent along with the Nez Perce by the agent at Lapwai to look after their behavior, helped prevent any possible trouble that might have developed.[48] The Shoshoni and Bannocks had James Dempsey in their party, a white man married to an Indian woman who had been with them a number of years. What influence he had with the tribes is not known.

Whites were happy that Chief Tendoy and fifty members of his Lemhi band were at the rendezvous. They knew that he was a restraining power in the Indian world and "one of the noblest

Chief Tendoy, chief of the Lemhi band, in 1883. (Courtesy of Museum of the American Indian, Heye Foundation, N.Y., neg. no. 22347)

Indians in America." The white officials hoped that Tendoy could be persuaded to give up the Lemhi country and move permanently to Fort Hall to assume the leadership of both the Shoshoni and Bannock tribes. He was the son of a Sheepeater mother and

Bannock father and seemed perfect for their plan. His attendance at this rendezvous, however, did more to hurt the Indian image and reputation than did all the biased news articles coming out of Boise and the acts of all the Indians in the area combined.

Picking up a supply of whiskey at Boise, Tendoy and his followers "had a grand drunk" when they reached the Payette. Tendoy was soon intoxicated and acted completely out of character. The chief told the settlers around the valley that the whites were deceiving themselves if they believed there was no danger. He warned them to "git up and git," and that the Indians intended to kill them all, men and women alike. He repeated "again and again" that Governor Bennett "talked, but would do nothing."[49]

The fear of apprehensive whites turned to anger, as many began to evacuate their families. They held meetings to discuss the possibility of a general outbreak of hostilities, and, on the upper Weiser, carefully eyed the huge encampment of Indians. But Tendoy's threats and actions aside, there was no trouble to the white settlers.

Three weeks after Tendoy's scare on the Payette, an anonymous letter signed by "Many Citizens" of the upper Weiser appeared in the *Statesman*. The letter pointed out that the citizens had sought the removal of the Weiser Indians "to the end that the raid[s] by other Indians might be stopped," but the settlers had been told by a military officer that the Indians must live somewhere. "The authorities," stated the letter, "could have sent a bottle of Mrs. Winslow's Soothing Syrup through here with much less expense, and with just as good an effect." With no assistance from the authorities forthcoming, these citizens threatened to take up arms if the Indians "make another raid" through their country and would help "insure their safe transit to their happy hunting ground."[50]

If the whites had tried to understand, they would have realized that the Indians had no intention of "raiding" the settlements. They had simply transferred their traditional lower Boise summer festival to the upper Weiser. Threats by whites and Indians alike were unfounded, and the great Indian rendezvous of 1872 was peacefully over by mid-August.[51]

This rendezvous was one of the largest ever held in southern Idaho after white settlement began in 1862. No "raids" had taken place, no homes or fields burned, and no trouble with the Indians in the upper Weiser were recorded. Peace had been maintained in spite of a malevolent minority on both sides.

FIVE

The Clouds of War

A RELUCTANT BAND

The authorities of Oregon and Washington, as well as the officials in Idaho Territory, were under increasing pressure to do something about the unsettled Indian population. In southeastern Oregon, bands of Paiutes and scattered Shoshoni groups, who had survived the Snake War a few years earlier, continued to roam through the countryside or took up residence at nearby army camps. On September 12, 1872, an executive order established the Malheur Indian Reservation for "all the roving and straggling bands in Eastern and Southern Oregon, which can be induced to settle there."[1]

By 1873 the 2,775-square-mile tract on the North Fork of the Malheur River was being settled by Chief Winnemucca's band, the Quinn River band under Natchez, the grandson of Chief Winnemuca, the Snake River band led by Egan, and those who followed Leggins, Ochoco, and Oytes. "Some Snakes under Eagle-eye mingled with them."[2] Eagle Eye and the main portion of the Weiser Shoshoni, however, remained in their old homeland, and even though they were the best of friends with Egan and the other Northern Paiute groups, they refused to settle on the reservation.

With Indian-white relationships in southern Idaho deteriorating, the white authorities believed that in order to preserve peace and protect the Indians from threatening groups of whites, the small bands who still held out should be moved as soon as possible to reservations. With the treaty period over, it was decided that the Shoshoni who inhabited southeastern Oregon, southwestern Idaho, and central Nevada were "Western Shoshones" and fell under the provisions of the treaty that had been held at Ruby Valley on October 1, 1863. Less than one-fourth of these Shoshoni had actually taken part in any treaty and had never received annuities. Furthermore, the Indians considered themselves "under no obligations to the General Government; and exhibit[ed] some reluctance to their proposed removal to a reservation."[3]

A special commission was created by the secretary of the interior to meet with the Shoshoni and Bannock of Fort Hall, but later instructions from the secretary directed the commission to contact the "scattered and wandering tribes" of the area.[4] General J. P. C. Shanks, an Indiana congressman, was named chairman of this commission, which also included Governor Bennett and Agent Henry W. Reed of the Fort Hall Reservation. It was soon obvious to this group that the worst trouble between Indians and whites was the "annoyance" the whites felt about roving groups of Shoshoni and Bannock. The commission's annual report for 1873 read, "the people of Idaho have the general dislike [of] Indians." In an attempt to induce the Indians to settle at the reservation, they visited not only the Weiser people to talk with Eagle Eye, but contacted "a number of tribes" that made up a population of about five hundred individuals northwest of Fort Hall.[5]

It should not have surprised the commission that Eagle Eye and his Weiser followers had no desire to submit to the life at the reservation. The Weisers were well informed by their Fort Hall friends of the sad conditions at the agency, the lack of food and scanty supplies that trickled in from the federal bureaucracy. Reed, yet another new agent, had arrived in January 1873, to find the same conditions that his predecessors had faced: He too was forced to send the fifteen hundred Shoshoni away from the reserve in order to keep them from going hungry.[6]

By early spring many groups had already departed for Camas Prairie and other points when word of a new Indian uprising sent a wave of hysteria through the West. The Modoc Indians had left the Klamath Reservation and had tried to return to their old lands. Led by Captain Jack (Kientepoos), this small group of Indians had resorted to war rather than return to the reservation in central Oregon. Word came from Fort Hall that there could be trouble there, for the Indians were "well informed" of the war and Captain Jack's movements.[7]

A *Statesman* reporter published the locations of various Indian groups in southwest Idaho that he thought might be tempted to join in the uprising. Dismissing half the Nez Perce that journeyed to the buffalo country beyond the Rocky Mountains, the paper pointed out that about that same number made annual visits to the Weiser country to "hold their pow-wows and hang around the outskirts of the settlements." The writer singled out the "murderous chief known as Eagle Eye" and the fifty warriors of his band on the upper Weiser, with a dozen more individuals located at the mouth of the river. Thirty or forty other Sheepeaters were located on the South Fork of the Salmon, east of Eagle Eye's location. Several smaller groups of Indians were noted on the Malheur, Boise, Owyhee, and Bruneau rivers. The same issue of the *Statesman* mentions that "the Committee of seven" were having petitions printed and sent to "different sections of the Territory for signers" demanding that the government "put the Indians on a reservation and keep them there."[8]

At Idaho City, the editor of the *Idaho World* agreed. Noting that the settlers in Payette and Weiser valleys were uneasy, he pointed out that in their area were three hundred Indians who were "insolent and defiant." Frustrated that the garrison did not have enough soldiers to "keep the guard house or mess room clean, let alone fight Indians," he urged that more soldiers be stationed at Boise.[9]

Eagle Eye and the Weiser people, more than any other group in southwest Idaho, were the target of white bitterness because their area was the site of the intertribal gatherings. By May, the *Statesman* was once again reporting that the Weisers were "very saucy" and frequently turned their horses into the settlers' grainfields. The Indians were accused not only of burning the grass and timber, but of setting fire to stacks of hay and fences. Indian Valley was a general "pow-wow ground" for all the "wandering tribes" in the country. "Of course," the editor had to admit, "they are not on the warpath, but they feel strong, and keep the settlers in constant dread and fear."[10]

To the whites, the military forces in Idaho were "contemptible," and they called for a company of militia to be formed in the capital. The purpose of the force was to deal with the young braves who "long to ornament their lodge poles with white men's scalps." Thirty-seven men, called the Payette Valley Home Guards, were organized at Falk's Store, near Emmettsville, while another group, the Horse Guards, formed at Warren. The Horse Guards were "one-hundred and twenty men fit for duty, if all could be found sober at once."[11]

When a small party of reservation Indians from Fort Hall passed through Boise Valley en route to the Weiser in the middle of May, the *Statesman* reported that the "pests" were making their "annual raids." The writer admitted that there was "probably" no reason for alarm, but it was prudent to be "on guard." The Modoc War was over by June, and the whites let the hysteria pass, much to the chagrin of at least one Weiser Valley citizen. He wrote:

> Rumour said that the Indians would not be permitted to trouble us another summer, but it was a mistake for they are all here this summer. . . . One big-bellied, sore-eyed monster, that amuses himself by going around among the women and children, telling them that they are to be burned up by and by. . . . Baptising Indians is all very well, but I would suggest that they be immersed, and the longer they are held under the better.[12]

Not all the settlers agreed with this writer. Most of them recognized that Eagle Eye and his Weiser people were peaceful and were not responsible for what little agitation was caused by other Indians. The Weisers were not only a source of laborers for the farms, but helped the whites by showing them how to preserve salmon, an important food source for Indians and whites alike.[13]

In October of 1873 the special commission returned to Fort Hall for a meeting with the Shoshoni and Bannock. The result of the meeting was an agreement restricting the Shoshoni and Bannock to the reservation and excluding possible conflicts with the whites. The success of the recommendations hinged on two main conditions: that Chief Tendoy and his Lemhi band give up their Salmon River country and move to Fort Hall, where it was hoped to place all the Indians under his leadership, and that Eagle Eye and the Weiser River band also be settled on the reservation.[14] Neither of the leaders had any desire or intention of moving to Fort Hall.

THE WHITES' LATER ATTEMPTS TO REMOVE EAGLE EYE

In the years following Eagle Eye's agreement to live peaceably and share the upper valleys with the whites, he managed not only to control his band, but evidently others who came there to hunt and fish as well. He also created good feelings between the Weisers and the local settlers. How he developed trust with the whites is not known, but however he did it, feelings of friendship began to replace suspicion.[15] Soon, prominent ranchers assumed the responsibility of handling local problems whenever they concerned white transgressions or horse stealing, and the local settlers began to recognize that of the other Indians, who only passed through the valley en route to the camas meadows or to fish at Payette lakes, "very few were bad Indians." Postmaster E. S. Jewell of the Salubria post office below Indian Valley stocked goods "to trade or 'swap' with the Indians who brought their furs, hides, robes, etc., to him for sale."[16]

The Weisers were also learning to trust the local whites. This growing friendly attitude between whites and Indians brought more of the shy Sheepeaters—as well as a few unhappy Bannocks and several Nez Perce members—under Eagle Eye's influence. By the late 1870s, the band numbered about one hundred and seventy members who recognized Eagle Eye as their leader.[17] One thing which helped strengthen friendly relations between the two races was the declining number of outside Indians who frequented the valley after the scares of 1872 and 1873.

Still, there were whites who saw the presence of the Indians as a threat, even though at that time no records existed of a white person being harmed by an Indian in the Weiser country. Much of the anti-Indian sentiment came from the Payette Valley, where a group of about twenty Bannocks, led by Bannock Joe, roamed the countryside committing petty depredations on the local settlers.[18]

Before Shanks and his special commission left Fort Hall late in 1873, they recommended that all the Bannocks and Shoshones of the Salmon River and southwestern Idaho be collected on the

Fort Hall Reservation. It was up to the local authorities to see that this was accomplished. Agent Reed, however, had more pressing matters at hand; by March 1874, stemming from charges of misconduct, he was under fire not only from white authorities, but from the Indian tribes as well. Still, he carried out the wishes of his superiors, and Eagle Eye was ordered to report to the Fort Hall Reservation with his band.[19]

Once again, Eagle Eye refused to accept the demands of the white authorities and ignored the orders. Governor Bennett was under pressure from the press and a hostile citizenry. Not only had he visited Eagle Eye's camp to urge the Weisers to go to Fort Hall, but the year before he had traveled to Washington to confer with the Commissioner of Indian Affairs. In Washington he had been asked to put his views in writing and file them with the department.[20] In a long letter to the commissioner on April 13, 1874, which in comparison illustrates the differences in whites' attitudes toward the Indians, he said:

> There is one band of Bannocks and Shoshones, under "Eagle Eye" that remain the whole year in Weiser Valley, in the midst of white settlers, hunting, fishing, stealing and marauding to the great danger and terror of the citizens. These Indians number over one hundred and by birth and Tribal relations properly belong on the Ft. Hall Reservation. Several smaller, and meaner bands are scattered along Snake and Bruneau rivers, to the great annoyance of the settlers there, and like those under "Eagle Eye" properly belong to the Ft. Hall reservation. . . . All these outside roving bands of Indians will without doubt continue to rove over the country, and will during each summer assemble in the Boise, Payette, and Weiser valleys, making "Eagle Eye's" band the nucleus and there meeting the Nez Perce, Umatilla, and other Indians from the North, hold high carnival for months, driving the settlers to the towns, and terrifying and exciting the whole country. Three times within the last three years this condition of affairs has happened, and a war was imminent, which if it had happened would have involved consequences more easily imagined than told. . . . The time has now arrived when the settlement of this question, in my judgement demands immediate action, if difficulty would be prevented, and the interests of the Territory—both whites and Indians—be protected. . . . The agents at Ft. Hall, Ft. Lapwai and at Umatilla Reservations should be required to prevent as far as possible all Indians under their control from leaving their reservations, except for business purposes and then in small parties, with passes. All roving bands

> should be at once peaceably notified to go upon the reservations to which by tribe and kindred they belong and in case of their refusal they should be forced to obey. . . . But in case of their obstinate refusal, to force them would be an easy task if properly managed. Especially should "Eagle Eye's" band of one hundred be immediately put upon Ft. Hall reservation—this is an easy task, and would break up the "Nest" on the Weiser, where year after year is hatched most of the troubles.[21]

Tendoy's band on the Lemhi was included in the list of independent groups Bennett wanted removed. Agent Reed was quick to point out that he had made the necessary preparations to receive all the groups at the agency, but that part of the fault for their failure to remove was due to "evil-minded or interested men" who encouraged them to stay, even "sympathizing with them in their fears."[22] By September, the Weiser and Lemhi Indians still refused to move, and Reed reported that the limited budget of the reservation was not enough to effect their removal.[23]

With this in mind, Governor Bennett and Idaho Delegate John Hailey sought a congressional appropriation to cover the expenses of gathering the nonreservation Indians to Fort Hall. When approved, $10,000 was made available, but Bennett was informed that the money was to be divided among the various Idaho agents and was not for the removal of Indians. With the sum being "barely sufficient, with the strictest economy to meet the necessary contingent expenses," the governor was left holding the Weiser citizens' petitions asking that the Weisers be removed to Fort Hall and no way to accomplish the removal.[24]

The Malheur Reservation to the west was to play an important part in the ensuing drama. When Agent Samuel B. Parrish had taken over in August 1874, he found only a few Indian families settled there, the rest having wandered away to hunt and fish for the summer. He set about winning native support in building up the reservation and establishing cooperation with the Paiutes under Egan and Leggins. Oytes, a prophet, was there with his followers, and created a few minor disturbances, but the operation of the reserve continued to progress into 1875.[25]

The Weisers were not the only Indians, still free, that the whites wanted on a reservation. It was reported of the Nez Perce that, "900 are vagrants in the Wallowa Valley and on the Snake and Salmon Rivers, where they have roamed for generations'' and would have nothing to do with a treaty, nor would they accept anything from the government. In Oregon, Joseph's band in the Wallowa Valley were holding out, in spite of having been ordered to the Nez Perce Reservation in June 1875, and having their lands opened to white settlement. In response to the government's actions, Joseph (Hin-mah-too-yah-lat-kekht, Thunder Traveling to Loftier Heights) called a council of the nontreaty leaders. This council was attended by the Snake and Salmon River chiefs. Eagle-from-the-Light, backed by White Bird (Pen-pen-hi-hi, white pelican), once again argued for an armed defense, but these two leaders were overruled and the group decided to remain at peace.[26] Tired of the threats of removal and the reluctance of the Indians to take action, Eagle-from-the-Light gathered his band and left to hunt buffalo with the Flathead people of Montana. He eventually settled on a reservation with his nephew, Duncan MacDonald, thus abandoning the Weiser country forever.

Eagle Eye's refusal to surrender to a reservation might have been reinforced that year when the government, by executive order, created the Lemhi Valley Indian Reservation for the ''mixed bands'' on February 12, 1875. Very likely, it was something he and the other Weisers would have welcomed happening in their own country, in spite of the problems other agencies seemed to be having. But news from the new reservation was as disheartening as it had been from the others. The new agent at Lemhi reported that the reserve was hit by an epidemic of whooping-cough whereby a great many had died and, by September, the Lemhi were reported as being ''very saucy and troublesome,'' possibly due to Mormon influence.[27]

The conditions at the Malheur agency were not much better even though ''700 Paiutes, Bannocks, and Snakes'' had spent the winter there and roving bands dropped in and out to receive food. There were no houses or shelter for the reservation Indians, the only tenements being ''skin, cloth, and tule lodges.'' Fort Hall Reservation was in better shape, but was shunned by the Weisers and Lemhis.[28] Still, the authorities were determined to move the Weiser and the Lemhi to Fort Hall even though the agency reported that the lack of food would force the reservation Indians already there to "rove and live as they [could] by stealing or begging."[29]

The embattled Agent Reed had been replaced at Fort Hall by James Wright, who reported, in January 1875, that he intended to send the Indians off the reservation just as his predecessors had been forced to do in previous years, even though he knew such action might antagonize the settlers.[30] His problems were exacerbated by local white authorities who pressured him to remove even more Indians to the neglected reserve.

Foremost in the whites' demands was the removal of Eagle Eye and the Weisers, who were reportedly "annoying" the whites. But Agent Wright was unable to budge the reluctant Indians from off their homeland. In the face of open criticism, he reported in April to the Commissioner of Indian affairs that he agreed that the Weiser Indians were "annoying the settlers," and he urged his superior to authorize him to send military troops to force their removal.[31] Before any action on his request could be put into effect, the frustrated agent resigned.

W. H. Danilson, a former agent at Fort Hall, was reappointed to the post in July. He immediately informed Washington officials of the disgusting conditions at Fort Hall and reported the few rations he did have would not feed the fifteen hundred Indians gathered there.[32] The change in agents and the pressing needs at Fort Hall overshadowed the problem of trying to remove the Weiser band to the agency for the rest of the year.

In the spring of 1876, the postmaster at Indian Valley, William Munday, reported that the valley now had eleven families—with thirty more on the Upper Weiser—and the area offered "many inducements to settlers and was fast settling up."[33] Many of the new arrivals had no use for Eagle Eye or his people. They saw the Indians as "retarding" the settlement of the region earlier in February. A petition was sent to Territorial Representative John Hailey stating

> that there is a roving band of Shoshone and Bannock Indians, numbering One hundred or more, under Eagle Eye as Chief, who make their head quarters near our settlement, and who annoy us very much by killing our cattle running at large, driving their stock into our grain fields without leave and by visiting our houses in large

> numbers during our absence from home and frightening our women and children. And that once or twice in each year the said Indians are visited by other bands who come in large numbers; and at such time they are especially annoying, and we are kept in constant apprehension of an outbreak and the settlement of the country is thereby retarded.
>
> We most respectfully ask that some person may be appointed to come and take charge of said Indians and to remove them to the Fort Hall Reservation, as the Agent at said Reservation is taking no steps in that direction, or to that end.[34]

Noticeably absent from the petition of thirty-four signatures were those of the original settlers still residing in the area. The petition was presented by Hailey to the Commissioner of Indian Affairs on March 3, 1876. Along with the petition he sent his own letter urging swift removal of the Weisers and recommended that the troops at Boise be dispatched to remove the Weiser Indians to Fort Hall.[35]

A few months later, on June 25, 1876, the nation was shocked to hear of the Battle of Little Bighorn and the massacre of General Custer's entire command in Montana. The story was told throughout Idaho, perpetrating another minor "scare" which lasted until the end of September. Idaho's acting governor, E. J. Curtis, who had replaced Bennett, requested additional troops to reinforce Fort Boise because the twenty-eight infantry troops were thought to be "no protection" against the "prowling bands who are now infesting" the upper Weiser and Owyhee countries. Curtis estimated the several bands in the area numbered from twenty-five to over one hundred "mounted and well armed" Indians who expected no resistance from the whites in the thinly populated rural districts. Enclosed with Curtis's request were letters and petitions he had received confirming that farmers were being accosted by the local Indians with "arrogant and brutal expressions" such as "How is Custer?"[36]

A rumor reached southern Idaho and Fort Hall that all the reservation Indians were to be shipped to Indian territory in Oklahoma. The word had been sent by the Utah Indians to the Shoshoni and Bannock bands, and the leaders had become so upset they had journeyed to Boise in July to meet with the governor to ascertain the truthfulness of the story.[37] If this story reached Eagle Eye on the Weiser, and it surely did, it could have only strengthened his resolve to resist going to the reservation.

The Indians at Malheur were quiet in spite of the fact that they were unhappy with the news that Agent Parrish was to be replaced. Egan and his Paiutes, who had been on the reservation for four years, had become good friends with Parrish, and things had been progressing well in spite of the presence of the medicine man, Oytes. By July 1, 1876, the number of Indians belonging to the reserve totaled 762. Winnemucca, while remaining a warm friend to the whites, still refused to come in, partially due to the presence of Oytes and his fear of starvation at the agency.[38]

Attempts to settle more of the roving bands on the reservation had been thwarted, in part by the great prophet, Smoholla, who lived at Priest Rapids on the Columbia. The hunchbacked leader was influential in urging resistance to white attempts to remove all nontreaty groups from their lands. Through his visions and dreams, he taught that the Indians would one day reinherit the earth and should remain in their ancestral villages living in the old ways. The new religion demanded that the "mother earth" should not be violated by "evil farming" like the whites were doing and that by holding out, the restoration of their lands from the whites would one day come to pass.[39]

While most of the Indian leaders in the northwest tribes were not directly influenced by the dreamer cult, many other leaders were. Dreamers like Oytes and Waltsac of the Paiutes, Toohoolhoolzote of the Nez Perces, Homily of the Wallawallas, and Talles of the Umatillas, were not only disciples of Smoholla, but held great sway among their respective peoples.[40]

THE NEZ PERCE WAR OF 1877

By the spring of 1877, the authorities were once more in a position to remove the nontreaty Indians to reservations. One of the first actions taken in that year was to clear the northern country of the nontreaty Nez Perce who had not moved to the Lapwai Reservation. Early in May, General O. O. Howard, military commander for the Department of the Columbia, was instructed to proceed, and he met with the Wallowa band under Joseph, the Salmon River band led by White Bird, and the band who followed Looking Glass. The old dreamer, Toohoolhoolzote, was the principal speaker. Negotiations broke down and the dreamer chief was put in the guardhouse. The Nez Perce were given thirty days to gather their cattle, horses, and belongings and be on the reservation. Leaving the Wallowa Valley, Joseph's band crossed the Snake and camped with White Bird at Tolo Lake, en route to the reservation. There, several of the frustrated young braves slipped away and killed four white men on nearby farms. This action forced their leaders into war.[41] In the face of the white push to round up the scattered native groups in western Oregon and Idaho Territory, the Indians began their final resistance for freedom and independence.

The news of the outbreak on the Salmon River had a devastating effect on the Weiser country. Whites and Indians alike were overwhelmed. White residents panicked and began defensive measures, and Eagle Eye and the friendly Weisers were suddenly suspect. Dispatches poured into Boise with news of the war, and letters from frightened settlers arrived requesting reinforcements. Hysteria gripped southern Idaho. The settlers organized local militia and hastily constructed forts at Emmettsville and other rural communities. Several stockades and fortifications were quickly erected on the upper Weiser.[42]

The community at Warren reported that they expected an attack "hourly" and were fortifying as best they could, though it was felt they could not stand much of a siege. They were certain of an assault: Indians had been seen "skulking around the mountains" nearby. Indian spies were reported on the upper Weiser by the stage driver, who also gave notice that the Weiser Indians had promised to come in but had failed to do so, creating some "excitement" there.[43]

Eagle Eye pointed out to his white neighbors that the Weisers were friendly and wanted nothing to do with the hostiles. Rumors circulated in Boise that some members of the band had already left to join the Nez Perce and that others were donning war paint. A private citizen named Milton Kelly, however, wrote the governor to reaffirm that the Weisers were peaceable and that they were all there except two, who were out hunting. Still, several "stray Indians" were reported in the area; three were "corralled" (one from Fort Hall and two from Malheur) and seven others passed by.[44]

White fears that the hostile Nez Perce would soon be reaching the valley were justified. John Hughes, a noted frontiersman of the time, summed up this view in a letter written to Territorial Secretary E. J. Curtis expressing the reasons why fear of attack was forthcoming:

> About this time of year each year they travel up the Little Salmon and cross into the North Payette Valley. In this valley there are each summer one thousand to fifteen hundred Indians, consisting of Indians from the lapway Reservation, Salmon River, Sheepeaters from the South Salmon, The Indian Valley band under Eagle Eye, Indians from the Fort Hall Reservation, some cayuses and Umatillas from Washington Territory. Joseph's band from the Walou [*sic*] valley and a few from the Malheur and Owyhee. They usually spend from one to three months in the valley, fishing, hunting, horse racing, gambling and trading. I do not think the whites trade with them there as I have always been told by the Indians that they got their supplies of ammunition, flour, etc. on the Weiser. I believe that this valley . . . will be where the Indians will have to be met and whipped.[45]

Hughes pointed out that it was advisable to notify all peaceable Indians not to roam about because the settlers were suspicious of them and might take matters into their own hands. Salubria's chief scout, F. J. Parker, noted that an outbreak of the Weiser Indians was possible: "Their actions are suspicious and for some weeks they have acted far different than usual," he reported. Any time a group of Indians were seen, the settlers of that locality were apprehensive.[46]

Eagle Eye's white friends wrote letters to the white authorities assuring them that the Weisers were peaceful. But the settlers were "in a fearful state of alarm constructing stokades and fortifications" and had deserted their farms and stock.[47] Armed riders patrolled the area.

As much or more apprehension had been created by this hysteria in the Indian camps, and the Indians began to fear for their own safety in the dangerous atmosphere. Eagle Eye must have anticipated contact with the Nez Perce, but he and his Weisers had no desire to join them in warfare. When members of the

Orlando "Rube" Robbins, center front, and his scouts. Robbins was to play a key role in pursuing the Weiser Indians during Idaho's three Indian wars. (Courtesy of Idaho State Historical Society)

band sighted four Nez Perce in the upper valley they did not wait to talk with them.[48] Instead, Eagle Eye called his group together and they decided to leave their country and head south to the Payette for safety.

Before the Indians departed, old Captain John called at the home of Ed Jewell's family, longtime friends of the Weisers, to pay a small debt. When told to let it go a few days, he refused, saying, "maybe no come again—pay now." The following morning not an Indian or camp was to be found; "they had gone silently during the night, under the cover of darkness."[49]

Several days later, "Rube" Robbins and his volunteer group of twenty-six Indian fighters who had been dispatched from Boise arrived on the upper Weiser. They were expecting to meet the Nez Perce in battle and at the same time to keep an eye on the Weiser Indians, in case they were inclined to join the hostiles. Robbins's report to Governor Mason Brayman on June 25, noted that the "friendly Indians had left the Weiser" and "no hostile act had yet been committed," but that there was much alarm in the community.[50] Much of the anxiety had been created by the sudden departure of Eagle Eye and his people from the area.

The Weisers crossed over to the Payette River where they made camp with their old friend, Chief Egan, near Emmettsville. A dispatch sent to the governor from Peter Pence, a stock raiser from Bluff Station, noted that the Weiser Indians had indeed made camp on the Payette, and they had told him that they had "left the Weiser to get away from the fighting." He mentioned that Egan had received a message from W. V. Rinehart, the new agent at Malheur, to return immediately, but that "Chief Egan seems stubborn and not conversent. Weisers say he stay 2 or 3 days maybe go one way and maybe another."[51]

Rinehart confirmed Pence's report in a message to Governor Brayman by informing Brayman that Egan and a small party of his Indians had left the reservation for a visit to Weiser river (their old home) just prior to the outbreak of Joseph's band, and they have not been heard from since." Fearing that they might have been induced to join the hostiles, he had sent a messenger after them.[52]

The Weisers were not welcome on the Payette. The whites there were as concerned for safety as the settlers on the Weiser had been. At the request of a number of citizens, the mail carrier, J. C. Shephard, wrote a letter to Brayman informing him that the Indians were "quite saucy" and "had no business roving around" there. He warned that there would be trouble if the "red devils" were not removed. The settlers, he said, would drive them off the river. "If they belong on the [W]eiser let them go there, for we don't want them here among us and will not allow it long."[53]

Robbins kept scouting parties in the upper country through the month of June. He was joined by Captain Bendier (no first name is recorded) and a company of forty-eight cavalry troops, who scoured the countryside for signs of the hostile Nez Perce force. Threatened by the local settlers, Chief Egan decided to follow Agent Rinehart's orders and return to the safety of the reservation. Egan managed to persuade some of the Weiser Indians to go with him, but Eagle Eye and twenty lodges of the band refused, preferring to wait out the uprising on the Payette. When the messenger returned to the Malheur, Rinehart dispatched the news to Brayman that Egan was en route with "seven lodges of his own and Weisers river Indians" and reassured him that the Indians belonging to his reserve posed no threat.[54]

The message from Rinehart evidently caused Brayman to realize the persuasive role Egan might play in persuading the Weisers to go to a reservation. It was well known that Egan was recognized as the leader in the area, and Rinehart hoped that with some negotiating, the rest of the Weisers might be convinced to go to the Oregon agency. On July 28, 1877, the governor wrote Rinehart requesting him to let Egan make another effort to convince Eagle Eye to go to the reserve. On August 7, Rinehart informed the governor that his letter had been turned over to William M. Turner, special agent for gathering straggling Indians to the reserve and that Turner would be going to the Weiser and Payette. He assured the governor that Turner would "spare no pains" to bring in all the Indians who could be induced to come.[55]

Eagle Eye's position on the Payette was precarious, even though the whites had learned, toward the end of July, that General Howard's troops had driven the hostile Nez Perce eastward. The settlers were upset when they saw the Indians arrive with "their horses dragging wickiups or carrying half-naked riders, the squaws wearing buckskin skirts carrying bundles of bedding and trumpery, the black-eyed children scampering here and there, and scroungy, barking dogs running about." Bannock Joe and his small group had already left the Payette country for the safety of Fort Boise, but Eagle Eye's Weisers were a much larger force and posed more of a threat.[56]

Eagle Eye and Bear Skin, a subordinate Bannock leader of rising importance, managed to keep the Weisers from traveling too far from their camp. It was not even safe to go hunting, for all Indians were under suspicion. One member of the band had been taken prisoner and accused of being a spy when he had headed into the upper Payette. He was put in jail in Boise.[57] With army patrols and militia groups combing the countryside and the settlers keeping close watch on them, there was little chance to gather winter supplies or reach the isolated safety of the mountains to the north.

When Eagan returned with Agent Turner, several weeks had passed since part of the Weiser band had departed with Egan and his Paiutes for the Malheur Reservation. The Weisers had evidently decided to wait out the white fears until they could return to their old camps in the upper country, but they met with the agent to hear what he had to say. Turner, with the help of Egan, who had relatives in the group, pointed out that "the government would soon place them on a reservation as a means of safety to themselves, even if it were necessary to use force for the purpose." Egan urged the Weisers to "come to the agency and share his home with him."[58] Eagle Eye relented, and Bear Skin and most of the band decided to come with him.

In his report to the Commissioner of Indian Affairs, Rinehart praised Turner's and Egan's accomplishment, noting that "through their combined efforts 139 Weisers, under chiefs Eagle Eye and Bear Skin, were induced to come to and accept Malheur Reservation as their future home."[59]

SIX

The Bannock War of 1878

A TROUBLED RESERVATION

The arrival of the Weiser River Shoshoni on the Malheur Reservation in August 1877, was heralded by Agent Rinehart as a breakthrough in the resistance of the few bands of Indians still roaming the countryside. Special Agent Turner was directed to visit Chief Winnemucca's camp on the Owyhee in southwestern Idaho. White authorities hoped that Turner could induce the old leader to return to the agency along with the others. Winnemucca and his subchief, Leggins, said there had been no blankets issued at Malheur the winter before and that he and his group still had no desire to return. Their main objection was the presence of Oytes the dreamer. They believed in his witchcraft, Turner said, and thought Oytes would practice his "evil enchantments until every Paiute except his own little band was driven from the agency."[1]

It was true that Oytes, the Smoholla-influenced prophet, lived there, but the Weisers recognized Chief Egan as the leader on the reservation. Egan's close association with the former agent and his knowledge of agency activities benefited the mixed bands in dealing with the whites. Even General Howard had a great respect for Egan. Egan had gained support from Oytes, and the two often confronted the agent together with complaints on reservation matters. Eagle Eye and Bear Skin, as well as the other headmen of the Weiser group, were content to follow Egan's able leadership.[2]

After Turner spoke with Winnemucca's band, he visited Waltsac, a non-treaty Columbia Indian located near the John Day Valley. He reported on October 4, 1877, that the chief professed friendship for the white "but insisted on his right to do precisely

Agent W.V. Rinehart of the Malheur Reservation. (Courtesy of Oregon Historical Society, neg. no. OrHi 56820)

as the whites do, living and going where he pleased'' and told the agent ''plainly'' that the band would not go to the reservation. Turner met with the same response from Ochoco's band at Surprise Valley, near Camp Bidwell. By December 17, Rinehart was able to report that Turner had ''tracked up'' the straggling bands of the region ''pretty thoroughly.'' He noted that they belonged to "Waltsac's band of non-treaty Indians at Priest Rapids, on the Columbia; to Ochoco's band, formerly of the Yainax Subagency; to Eagle Eye's band of Shoshones in Idaho, and to Winnemucca's band in Nevada."[3]

The failure to lure Waltsac, Winnemucca, and Ochoco to the agency during 1877 raised many questions for Agent Rinehart to consider. In outlining some of the possible reasons to the department in Washington, he noted "that while 139 of the Weisers, who never tried reservation life before, have been brought upon the reservation by Mr. Turner, few of Winnemucca's and none of Ochoco's people, who have formerly been upon reservations, could be induced to return." He felt there were three reasons the Indians would not return: "defects in the reservation system, lack of sufficient means to administer the system," and "mismanagement by the Indian Bureau and its agents."[4]

The problems he cited were real, but worse than they appeared on paper. Soon after Rinehart arrived, he established policies that alienated the native population, and a rift developed between him and the Indian leadership. Rinehart had announced that the reserve did not belong to the Indians, but to the government, and that the Indians would be paid a dollar a day for labor. From these wages, Rinehart told them, they could buy food and clothing (items which—the Indians felt—were sold at inflated prices). When the Indians objected to the policies, Rinehart said that if they did not like the way he ran the reservation, they could all leave. Egan and his leaders were forced to go to the military authorities with their complaints.[5]

Rinehart's integrity and effectiveness as the agent at the Malheur Reservation was certainly open to question.[6] Sarah Winnemucca, the outspoken interpreter at the agency, was dismissed amid rumor and charges she had made that the teacher and other employees were fleecing the Indians at cards. Rinehart himself had beaten an Indian almost to death. It was also suspected that Rinehart was conniving with residents of Canyon City to open the reservation to white settlement.[7]

Rinehart, in his own defense, cited financial problems. He said that if given "$12 a year for clothing to each person, $6,000 a year for lumber, tools, implements, teams, traveling and in-

Oregon Indians typical of those found on the Malheur Reservation. (Courtesy of Oregon Historical Society, neg. no. OrHi 8227)

cidental expenses and transportation, and $6,000 for pay of employees," as department regulations prescribed, $80,000 per annum would be required to run the agency, but the congressional appropriation for the year had only been $15,000. His supplies of clothing and food, made available in March, had not arrived until November 14, 1877, and the winter was spent without medical supplies. He reported that the department's "Circular No. 10," relating to Indian labor, was one of the chief causes of discontent on the reservation. Six of the directives listed in the circular, he told the commissioner, had created problems for him and the Indians: 1) the possibility that beef and flour would no longer be issued; 2) the requirement that they farm, but that no tools be given them; 3) reduced wages; 4) the requirement that they exchange their horses for cattle, sheep, and hogs; 5) a ban on the sale of ponies to Indians; 6) a prohibition on other Indians visiting.[8]

The Weisers found the reservation a safe refuge, but unappealing. It was simply a piece of land with a few agency buildings onto which hundreds of Paiutes, Bannocks, and Shoshonis had been herded. It lacked the rudimentary necessities for

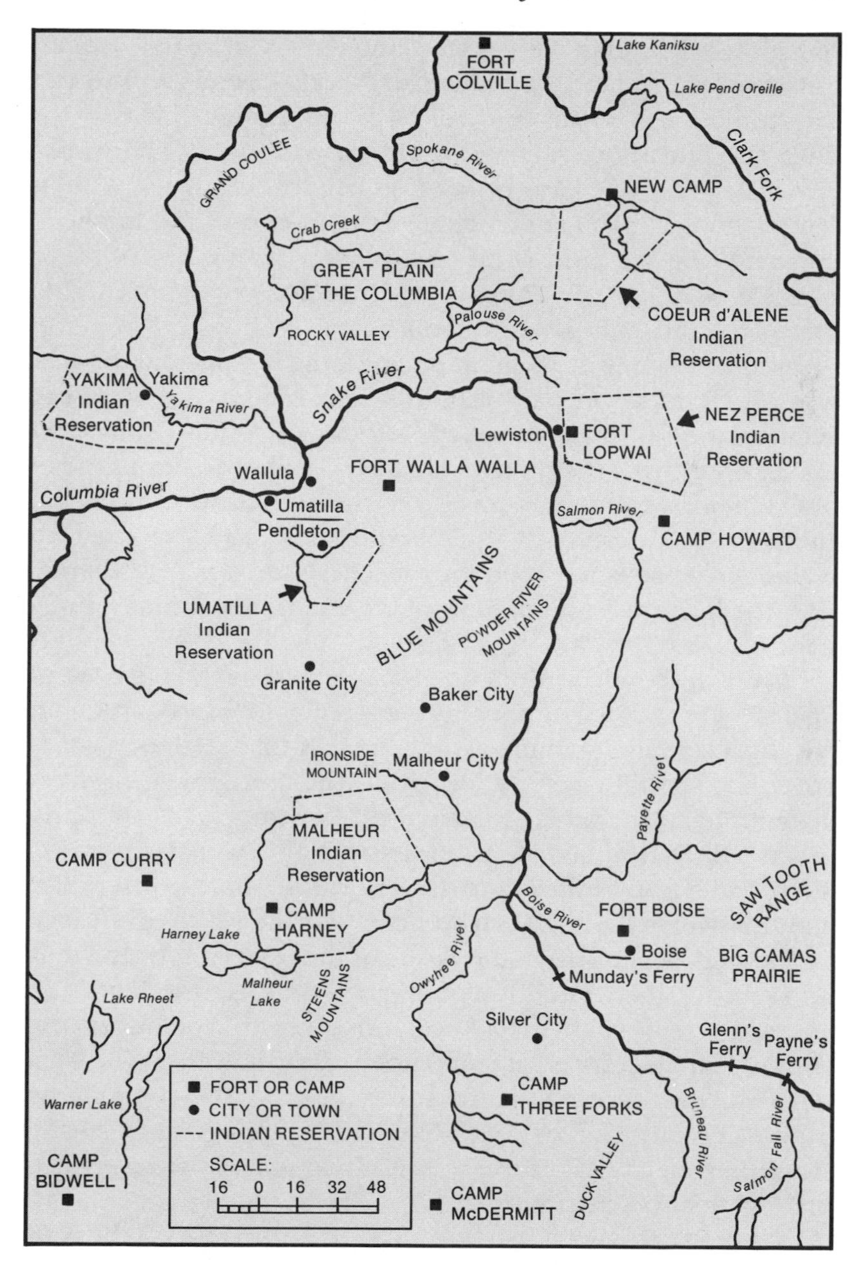

The Bannock War of 1878. (Based on "Plan of Operations, Department of the Columbia, 1878," U.S. Department of War, Executive Division, General's Office, Annual Report, 1878)

living the white man's life-style—and that is what the Office of Indian Affairs wanted the Indians to do. The agent's attitude was the same as that of the OIA. His "central thought" was to "induce the Indians to labor in civilized pursuits." The Indians remonstrated: "We have no wagons or plows to work with; no fences, no teams to haul fencing with; no houses, no lumber to make houses; we must soon feed ourselves. We have to work *now* for what we get. Farmers and cattle-men pay us $1 a day for work, and you pay only half as much."[9]

Another source of agitation between the Indians and the agent was over horses. Rinehart unsuccessfully tried to discourage the accumulation of what he called "worthless ponies" and wrote his superior that "the Indian character—full of roaming and exploits in horsemanship—developes their greed for this favorite species of property. All their acquired wealth—women and wampum—is lavished upon the one cherished object of their desire, the horse. . . . Indeed, they are the Indians' highest standard of value."[10]

Many of the accusations against Rinehart may have been unjust. He was accused of opening the agency to white settlement, but this may have stemmed from the fact that settlers were encroaching upon the reservation. Still, white settlement could not be ignored and Rinehart reported on December 18, 1877, that it was "likely to produce future trouble." Twenty trespassers alone had "1,400 horses and 10,839 cattle" on the reservation and the whites had "grown so bold that they have even taken up their residence within the limits of the reservation, and make no secret of their intention to occupy and use the land." His attempt to remove them had been unsuccessful and he reported that without military aid it could not be accomplished. The squatters had been ordered off the reservation by the commanding officer at Camp Harney, but none had complied. They had, instead, moved to cut off the western portion of the reservation and open it to settlement.[11]

Eagle Eye spent a harsh winter with his people on the reservation. The rift between the Indians and the agent deepened. By spring 1878, the band had had enough. In the middle of March, "nearly all the Weisers" decided to return to their homeland and rejoin their people holding out in the mountains. Rinehart was not surprised; it was "usual for them to scatter out from the agency in early spring for the purpose of hunting, fishing, and root-digging."[12]

They were ill-received on the Weiser. The whites were already moving in to homestead the vacated meeting grounds in Council Valley, a few miles north of the Weisers' old winter camps at Indian Valley.[13] There was no longer a place for them, and they knew that to stay could mean open hostilities between themselves and the whites. More distressing were the rumors of another possible outbreak by their old friends to the east at Fort Hall. Bannock emissaries had visited the Malheur agency "early in the season to tell their grievances" and to warn of future troubles. The Bannock intended to go to Camas Prairie "when the grass came" and then "go to the buffalo country to fight the soldiers."[14]

On April 14 Rinehart reported that a serious confrontation between himself and "all the chiefs except Winnemucca" had taken place over a Bannock rumor. The chiefs had heard that their horses were to be taken from them and the Indians were to be disarmed by the soldiers. When it was denied, Rinehart and his interpreter were accused of conspiring against them. Indian fears stemmed from a January affair at Fort Hall when three companies of cavalry had surprised a village of Bannocks, seized their weapons, and confiscated nearly three hundred horses.[15]

On April 23 Rinehart reported that Indians "from all parts of the country" were gathering on the reservation. He noted that more Indians were there than at any time during the winter, and said he was suspicious because in the spring they usually scattered. He said that the Weisers had "returned from Idaho bringing with them 30 more who have never been there before." He attributed this unrest to the difficulties at Fort Hall and noted that while "it was not indicating hostilities on the part of these people, it must be taken as an index to their fears, and the conviction on their part that there is real trouble abroad in the near future."[16] By the end of April he reported that 551 Indians had come onto the reservation.[17]

The agents at Fort Hall and Malheur expressed growing concern of the situation in the Snake country, but the citizens of

Buffalo Horn. (Courtesy of Idaho State Historical Society)

the area showed little regard for signs of trouble. On March 5, 1878, the *Statesman* noticed that the "Indians bumming" around Boise City were buying ammunition from citizens. The editor thought it was "criminal" for the whites to sell it to them. The possibility of trouble did not stop the paper from extolling the settlement of Camas Prairie, guaranteed to the Indians by treaty as part of their reservation. The "extremely fertile acres," reported the editor, "possesses [*sic*] too many inducements to settlers to remain much longer unoccupied."[18]

By early May, about two hundred Indians had congregated near Payne's Ferry on the Snake River. They were reported to be very "saucy." Buffalo Horn, a rising leader and noted scout who had served with the army during the Nez Perce War the year before, was trying to control them. In mid-May Buffalo Horn visited Boise where the "loyal" Bannock received permission from Governor Brayman to buy two dollars worth of ammunition for deer hunting.[19] He also received a pass to visit the Umatilla Reservation in Oregon.

En route to that agency, the young warrior stopped at Malheur. He was later reported as inciting the Indians at Malheur to join the Bannocks should there be an uprising. Chief Egan decided to accompany him to the Umatilla agency, where they spent three days.[20]

In Nevada, Agent A. J. Barnes reported that Bannock messengers had been dispatched to Pyramid Lake, but the Paiutes there refused to join them. The reply to the Bannocks was the same from the Duck Valley Shoshonis, though the Bannocks had warned them that "when they had destroyed the railways and killed the whites, they would divide both sides of the world among their friends, and kill all Indians who had not united with them."[21]

Things were "all quiet" at Malheur on May 25, and "very few" Indians were on the reservation itself, although a party of thirty warriors were sighted escorting a group of squaws with papooses. The Indians had moved down the Malheur River some twenty-five miles and were encamped with Bannock Jack's band from Fort Hall. Sarah Winnemucca, the influential daughter of Chief Winnemucca, was sent for by the Indian leaders. When she arrived she met with Chief Egan who requested her help in presenting their complaints against Rinehart to the authorities. Before she could act, the time for negotiations with the white authorities ran out.[22]

THE GREAT INDIAN FEDERATION

Early on June 1, "Chief Eagle Eye and about 45 of his Weiser people" arrived at the agency to draw their rations and "left immediately going east." Rinehart reported that the forty-six visiting Bannock at the Malheur Reservation were refused rations, though Chief Egan pleaded for them. The chief divided his own rations with them and both parties "left at once" toward the Snake River. The day following Eagle Eye's departure, a courier arrived from Fort Boise en route to Camp Harney with a report that hostilities had broken out at Camas Prairie. One man was killed and another wounded.[23]

Although apprehensive at the news, Rinehart said that the Indians of Malheur had given "no hint of their designs, no evidence of hostile intent." Rinehart had learned that "all the tribes" were congregating at the fish traps on the main Malheur River, twenty miles away. His attitude began to change, however, when, on June 5, his five native employees suddenly left "without saying a word." Two days later the Indians failed to arrive to draw their rations and he concluded that "they were intent on mischief" and decided to abandon the agency.[24]

At Camas Prairie, where Buffalo Horn met the Fort Hall bands and Tendoy's Lemhis, white man's hogs were again destroying the camas fields. Cattle as well had been driven into the area by local ranchers. The government authorities had not enforced the treaty; they had not stopped the settlers from encroaching on the camas grounds. Indian patience was at an end. On May 30, 1878, several young warriors attacked a camp of three whites, critically wounding two before the whites escaped. One author wrote that he "must admit that the Indians under their code of morals and government, had ample justification for the methods they pursued."[25]

Buffalo Horn and two hundred of the Bannock warriors decided for war. Tendoy's band and the Fort Hall Boise Shoshoni, under Captain Jim, chose peace, and decided to return to their reservations. Buffalo Horn led his group south and west toward the Owyhee and Oregon, where they hoped to be reinforced by the Northern Paiute and other reservation Indians. At King Hill, southeast of Camas Prairie, Buffalo Horn plundered freight

Captain Reuben F. Bernard. (Courtesy of Idaho State Historical Society)

wagons, then crossed the Snake River at Glenn's Ferry, cutting the ferry adrift behind them. When they reached Bruneau Valley, they killed several settlers, but found that others had fortified themselves. With the troops from Fort Boise, under Captain R. F. Bernard, and the civilian scouts, under Orlando Robbins, in close pursuit, Buffalo Horn pushed up the Bruneau River toward Malheur.[26]

The Camas Prairie outbreak came as no surprise to the Indians assembled at Malheur. While Rinehart was busily engaged in deserting the agency, the various bands were deciding on peace or war. Most of Winnemucca's Paiutes wanted peace. Others, like Paddy Capp's band, had already agreed to join the hostiles. "Their spirit prophets, for example, Oytes of the Malheurs, prophesied that the time had come when the Indians were to destroy the whites and recover their country."[27] Egan proposed peace, until be became convinced that his Paiutes were for war. He knew "they would be subdued—but he would fight as long as he could, and then he thought the Great Father at Washington would give him more supplies, like he did when they quit fighting before, and not try to make his people work."[28]

The Weisers faced a moral and ethical dilemma that threatened the band. Bear Skin and his Bannock element chose war and were reinforced by War Jack (Tamanmo), part Bannock and part Nez Perce, who was visiting from Fort Hall and was forced by the unrest to stay. Eagle Eye, as their senior leader, was faced with the final decision. According to family sources, he was enough of a diplomat to decide against the Bannocks and avoid impending hostilities, and probably used his influence on his followers as well. But for many of the Indians there were few alternatives. Their homelands had been claimed by the whites and there were threats of Bannock reprisals for all who refused to join. If the majority of the Weiser people were for retribution, it was understandable. They were a displaced people who had been driven from their land, and the whites had threatened them against returning. Egan and Oytes pointed out the injustice of the whites, and those still undecided wavered. Agent Rinehart had no doubt about which way the Indians would decide. He reported that the "250 warriors" on the reservation would join the hostiles.[29]

A Bannock chief in full regalia. (Courtesy of Oregon Historical Society, neg. no. OrHi 10099)

The Malheur Indians moved to Juniper Lake, west of Steen's Mountain, to meet for another council with Buffalo Horn's Bannocks and the Paiute band under Chief Winnemucca. The Bannocks arrived in a state of excitement with news of a battle near South Mountain in southwestern Idaho on June 8. Buffalo Horn and a war party of sixty handpicked warriors had been attacked by a group of white volunteers from Silver City. The Indians had killed two whites and wounded three others, and Buffalo Horn had been mortally wounded. After several days' travel he asked to be left behind to die.[30]

There were "more than 300 lodges and 450 warriors" assembled at the camp at Juniper Lake, and the Bannocks among them were furious. When Winnemucca refused to join the hostile Bannocks, he and his followers were held prisoners. Sarah Winnemucca sneaked into the camp and helped the old chief and about seventy-five of his followers escape.[31] On reaching Bernard's camp on the Owyhee, Winnemucca reported to the captain that the hostiles intended to head north to contact the Umatilla and Columbia River Indians. He said the hostile force was "composed of the Bannocks, Eagle Eye's band of Weisers, and Oit's [Oytes] band of [P]iutes" with Oytes in command over all. After Buffalo Horn's death, Egan had become a reluctant leader and he and his band were being held as prisoners until they could be armed.[32] Within days, however, it was learned that "Egan at last consented to be their war-chief."[33]

Paiute Chief Natchez and his band fled to the whites from Juniper Lake. He reported that originally the number of hostiles did not exceed "thirty lodges of Bannocks and Eagle Eye's band of Weisars [*sic*], and a party of Snakes, some of whom were determined to escape at the first opportunity."[34] The hostile ranks were swelling as "Indian runners were going from tribe to tribe"[35] and others rushed to join them. News reached the settlements that a few of the Klamaths and Umatillas had joined the alliance and the "hostiles were increasing as they advanced." Some of the Columbia River Indians had also decided to go to war and "a number of Moses [Que-tal-a-ku] Indians [Sinkiuse tribe] were with them."[36]

General Howard, commander of the Department of the Columbia, later reported that the Bannock raiding party had been "comparatively small until re-enforced, as I now know, by all the Malheur Indians."[37] When news of the outbreak first reached him in Portland, he wasted no time mobilizing and dispatching troops to the field. In the white settlements volunteer companies of civilians were being organized in response to reports of Indian movements. The hostiles were moving fast, plundering and raiding, as they headed toward sympathetic friends in the Umatilla and Cayuse lands. Bernard and Robbins were the only white force in close pursuit.

News that the Weiser Indians had joined the hostiles was anticipated by many of the whites in Idaho. On June 15, 1878, the editor of the *Statesman* warned that though he did not want to "excite the fear of anybody," the Indians' purpose was to steal and murder. He prophesied they would raid the Bruneau, Malheur, and Weiser countries in order to take revenge on the settlers "who occupy their most coveted old grounds." Another item in the same issue of the *Statesman* predicted that raids were likely on the Payette and Weiser if the Indian army were to break into small bands. But the settlers on the Payette were already on alert. It had been reported that Indians had been sighted near the Payette, and the whites in the valley were building a fort at Falk's Store. The settlers on the Weiser followed suit. They were building one fort on the Weiser and another on Mann's Creek. Their volunteer company of sixty men assigned ten scouts to watch the Snake and Old's Ferry.[38]

On June 21, Robbins and his scouts located the hostile force at Silver Creek, northwest of Harney Lake. He estimated their number at two thousand with more than half warriors. "If the estimate proved to be correct, it meant that this was the largest concentration of warring Indians since the massacre of Custer and his troopers by the Sioux."[39] In a daring daylight attack on June 22, 1878, the scouts and part of the command charged through the enemy camp. They hoped to surprise and confuse the Indians. The remainder of Bernard's troops blocked off the lower part of the village. Yelling, "with six-shooter and carbine" blazing, Robbins and his men charged twice through the camp before the Indians could group. While the warriors climbed the bluffs to fortified positions above the village, "a line of skirmishers of the enemy, composed principally of the chiefs and sub-chiefs'' met the troopers. ''Several hand to hand encounters were observed,'' the ''most noticeable being between Bear Skin, a Bannock Chief, and Sergeant Geo. H. Richmond'' who shot the warrior.[40]

Chief Egan secured a horse, rode bravely into the melee and charged at Robbins. Egan ''had a repeating rifle, and when within a few steps of Col. Robbins, he would fire at him, throw himself on the opposite side of his horse and rise quickly to fire again.'' Robbins finally ''sent a bullet through one of Egan's wrists, which broke it'' and the chief fell to the ground where he was shot again in the breast. Before the leader could be carried off by his warriors, he was wounded near the groin by another scout.''[41]

The wounding of Egan intensified the fighting, and the troops were forced to pull back from the battlefield. They waited for the arrival of General Howard's command. The whites had lost three men and three others were seriously wounded, but Indian casualties were indefinite. Bernard's column numbered less than three hundred men, including Robbins's militia. Bernard estimated the Indian force at near two thousand.[42]

Oytes assumed command of the Indian force and convinced them to strip off their baggage and continue north where ''they would find allies among the Umatillas and other Indians.''[43] Though badly wounded, Egan directed a retrograde movement and crossed over into the John Day Valley with the army in pursuit and Robbins's scouts dogging their trail. The advance guard of Indians met and defeated a party of volunteers in a running fight on June 29 at Murder's Creek, and the Indian's rearguard left an ambush on the North Fork of the John Day, which was discovered by the scouts before the troops arrived. The Indians moved fast, killing settlers, slaughtering and mutilating livestock, and destroying ranches. Though the troops managed to overtake and engage them at several locations, the whites could not stop them. Citizens at Canyon City and Prineville panicked when news arrived that the hostile force might be heading in their direction. They erected fortifications and sent for volunteer reinforcements,[44] but the Indians bypassed the white towns in their effort to reach their Umatilla friends and the Columbia River. A volunteer force from Pendleton engaged several hundred of the hostiles and were nearly annihilated. The Indians moved on into the high country between the John Day and Grande Ronde rivers.

Army scouts located Egan's forces on Birch Creek. Howard's troops attacked on July 8, driving the Indian army into the pine forests of the Blue Mountains, but the hostiles continued their trek toward a rendezvous with the Umatillas. Howard acted quickly with troop movements. He ordered steamers to be outfitted as gunboats. They were to patrol the Columbia and Snake rivers and prevent the Indians from crossing and joining the Yakima and other Indians in Washington.[45]

Captain Evan Miles and his command of five hundred soldiers used forced marches to reach the Umatilla Reservation ahead of Egan's forces. Arriving at the agency on July 12, 1878, Miles learned that some of the Indians had already "went over to the Snakes." Miles was attacked by an element of Egan's followers who came down from the hills while the troops were eating breakfast. The Umatillas, led by Chief Umapine (Wa-kiu-kou-we-la-sou-mi), were in war paint and feathers and sat watching the battle from a hilltop. The battle lasted all day, until at nightfall the Indians retreated. Five warriors had been killed, and the Umatilla leaders came in that night to negotiate with Captain Miles.[46]

When the settlers across the Snake River in Idaho heard news of the battle, they were frightened. Howard's engagement at Birch Creek and Miles's fight at the Umatilla had stopped the Indians' move west, and their northerly progress had been effectively checked by the gunboats on the Columbia. General Howard had anticipated that the Indians would turn in the direction of the Wallowa and Weiser countries, so on July 11 he had ordered Captain Harry Egbert and a battalion of soldiers to Indian Valley with instructions to scout toward Payette Lakes in order to cut off "returning hostiles."

In Boise the Indian force was said to be comprised of "a portion of the Bannocks, the Piutes of the Malheur Reservation, the Weisers, and a few other roving bands, with perhaps a few of the Nez Perce and some renegades from the Upper Columbia." But more alarming to the whites of Boise was the news that since the Indians had been turned toward Idaho, they would probably be "crossing the Snake river to the North and passing through the Weiser country." A letter from Weiser Store informed the *Statesman* readers that families were leaving the area and they did not expect to have "enough men left for a corporal's guard."[47]

The situation on the upper Weiser was intense, the settlers there in a near panic. Captain A. J. Borland of the territorial militia had arrived the second week of July. He found people "greatly excited all along the Weiser" and in a "deplorable condition." They had fortified themselves in the center of the valley. "I have seen considerable excitement caused by Indian troubles," he reported, "but never have seen anything that equals this."[48] He made the fort his headquarters and immediately set about organizing the men into two companies, one of home guards and one of mounted minutemen.

Anxiety had been heightened when the *Statesman* had warned on July 11 that, while it did not want to "alarm the people there unnecessarily," the Weiser settlers should be on guard. The hostile force, the editor speculated, might pass through the valley, giving the "Weiser Indians the opportunity of punishing the people there for supposed grievances."[49]

The fear of imminent attack was justified. T. C. Galloway, commissioned as captain in the local militia, confirmed the situation in the Weiser Valley and noted that the valley was "home to two of the prominent hostiles, Egan and Eagle Eye." In a blast at the governor, he appealed for arms and ammunition and mentioned that previous requests were "not even so much as answered by his Excellency, Gov. Brayman." In the meantime, the fort had been reinforced with firing pits and trenches in case the settlers were put under siege. The citizens of Boise formed a volunteer group ready to head for Weiser Valley at the first sign of an attack.[50]

THE END OF THE ALLIANCE

After the battle with Captain Miles on July 14, Chief Egan led the Indian forces into the Blue Mountains to regroup and await the arrival of the Umatilla allies. Within several days a large party of warriors—led by chiefs Umapine, Five Crows (Pak-ut-ko-ko), and Yettinewitz—made their appearance at the Indian camp to talk with Egan. Unknown to the hostile leaders, the Umatillas had negotiated with the army officers to kill or capture Egan. In return for the betrayal, Chief Umapine was to be forgiven by the army for attempting to join the Indian league, and tribal members already with the alliance were to be pardoned.[51]

In the discussion between Egan and the Umatillas, the Umatillas pretended friendship and managed to lead Egan and seven of his followers out of camp.

There are several versions of what happened next. At a prearranged signal the Umatillas opened fire, killing Chief Egan and thirteen of his followers. Several ''Malheurs'' were taken as prisoners.[52]

Before the warriors in camp could retaliate against the treachery of the Umatilla party, Umapine and his warriors had retreated with several scalps, including Egan's. Egan's group now faced not only a persistent white army that was rapidly closing in, but the entire Umatilla nation. Further, the cavalry columns to the north were being aided by Nez Perce scouts.[53] Egan's followers knew, surely, that the death of their leader signaled the end of a succession of leaders capable of welding together the Indian federation. The Bannocks ''laid the blame on Oits [*sic*] and his band, who, they claimed, had misled them, in the belief that they would find allies among the Umatillas,'' and they resolved to return to buffalo country.[54] Though not subdued, the loss of so many principal men forced the Indians to break their alliance. The different bands struck out on their own in an attempt to return to their homes.

The Weisers' leaders gathered together their families and whoever chose to follow them. They decided to try to reach their homeland in the Weiser country. They broke camp at once, certain that the Umatilla traitors would report their location to the military troops. Their trail was ''strewn for six miles with large quantities of provisions and, to them, valuable supplies.''[55]

Colonel Wheaton had arrived at Captain Miles's camp at the agency when the victorious Umatillas brought in Egan's scalp. Not trusting the information, Wheaton sent Colonel Robbins and a small party to the massacre site, located several miles southeast of Meacham Station. Robbins returned the next day with the head and wounded arm of the war chief, confirming Egan's death. Robbins reported that the hostiles' camp had been deserted and that two of the Indian trails appeared to be heading toward the Grande Ronde or Powder rivers. Wheaton dispatched 97 Umatilla Indians under Chief Umapine, accompanied by three white scouts, to pursue the hostiles. Lieutenant Colonel Forsyth, newly arrived from General Sheridan's headquarters, took command of Bernard's battalion and followed the trail behind the Umatilla allies.[56]

The Weisers' trail led past Starkey's ranch and Daley's road, toward the head of Birch Creek. Even though they had discarded most of their supplies and extra horses, they were encumbered with women and children and could not outdistance the Umatillas. On July 17, 1878, at two in the afternoon, Chief Umapine and his warriors overtook the struggling band on the East Fork of Birch Creek. In a surprise attack, the Umatillas "charged them, killed seventeen bucks, captured twenty-five women and children, and sixty or seventy head of stock."[57] One of the fallen warriors was reported to be Eagle Eye.

When Forsyth arrived at the scene the Weisers had been shattered, broken into small parties and "getting off as fast as possible." Shortly after the army troops arrived, the Umatilla "returned with their trophies to their reservation." Under interrogation the captured women said the Indians were intending "to try and make their way over into the Weiser country, and thence to Bannock or Buffalo country." This information was dispatched to Colonel Wheaton who now sought to "prevent any organized bands of hostiles from moving toward the Weiser country." With guards at Cayuse Station, Meacham's, and Pelican, Wheaton directed Major Sanford with his squadron and Nez Perce scouts to head west and "intercept any bands of hostiles coming that way en route to Weiser."[58]

The Morning Oregonian in Portland made front-page news of Eagle Eye's death. A letter from Olive Creek, eastern Oregon, dated July 22, 1878, informed the readers that Colonel Forsyth and Captain Bernard had passed by with the news that "Eagle Eye was killed some four days ago."[59] While many whites breathed a sigh of relief over the information, others were skeptical.

The settlers on the Weiser remained fortified, with scouts closely watching the area around Brownlee Ferry. They welcomed the news of the arrival of Major Egbert's force in Indian Valley. With Egbert watching and scouting the Weiser and Payette country, and Forsyth, Sanford and other columns pressing the Indians at Ladd Canyon, the Grande Ronde, and Burnt River Meadows, the *Statesman* reported that the Weiser country was "well guarded."[60]

By July 27, 1878, General Howard had received enough information from his field officers to determine that the Indians were in full retreat. The fact that the Indian forces had been broken into scattering groups was evident from their many trails. He concluded

> that the Indians had broken up into very small bodies and were moving, some southward toward Stein's [*sic*] Mountain, some in the opposite direction, toward the Weiser region, and some on the routes across the Owyhee, I believed that the Piutes and Weisers would not go far from their old homes, while the Bannocks would endeavor to get to Lemhi and Fort Hall, or perhaps carry out their insane project of going to the buffalo country and thence to Sitting Bull.[61]

His observations were correct. Within days, Ochoco and sixty of his warriors came in from Steen's Mountain to surrender at Camp McDermitt. Ochoco was followed by Oytes, the old dreamer and medicine man, who brought his followers to the Malheur Reservation, where they were held prisoners. The Bannocks emerged from the Owyhee the first week in August, and the military force on the Weiser headed south to intercept them.[62]

News in Boise in August 1878, read that "old Eagle Eye, Chief of the Weiser Indians, is surely killed." Returning scouts verified his death at the hands of the Umatillas, and one had even "turned him over and took a good look" at the fallen leader.[63] The news did not console the settlers on the Weiser. They were left with little protection and, within days of Major Egbert's departure, reports of Indian sightings began to come in.

Reports of Eagle Eye's death at the hands of the Umatillas on Birch Creek might have come as a surprise to the Weiser leader as well as to his family, if they had known. According to the oral traditions of his descendants, and supported in later years by white friends, the wily old fox survived to lead his four sons and their families to safety. This entire extended family moved into the wilderness of southwestern Idaho, where they spent some time, at least, the following winter.[64]

Following the attack at Birch Creek the Weiser families broke into small parties and scattered eastward under several headmen and important warriors. Each group made its way through the unsettled high lands east of Powder River Valley and crossed the Snake River into the mountains of their old homeland.[65] Andy Johnson's Sheepeaters headed for their homes on the South Fork of the Salmon River, while another group of Weisers, led by Bouyer, united with War Jack (Tamanmo) and some of his Fort Hall Bannocks and decided to reach the sanctuary of the rugged Middle Fork. General Howard noted that a "few Weisers [had] gone into the rough country between the Weiser and Snake" and eventually made their way into the Seven Devils Mountains.[66] This was probably Eagle Eye's group. Indian Charley, the Nez Perce headman, lead his followers into the high country to avoid the possibility of being discovered by the whites. Other small parties of Weisers attempted to reach relatives at the Lemhi.

Captain A. J. Borland's volunteers surprised a small camp of "Weisers and Nez Perces" that resulted in the capture of one of the women, six horses, a quantity of venison, buffalo robes, and other items.[67] The Weiser citizens believed that the entire country was about to be "overrun by the red fiends" because sightings were made with, what was to the citizens, alarming frequency. Indians were reported crossing at all points between the mouth of the Weiser River and Connor Creek. The mountains were "getting full of them."[68] Borland returned to Boise on August 7, and reported that several bands, numbering over a hundred, were in the Weiser area.

The situation was convoluted. White thieves and raiders were taking advantage of the Indian war by making moccasin tracks and passing out false reports in order to keep the settlers occupied while their stock were stolen. In a stern warning, the Payette settlers threatened that any person "playing Indian" would be "shot on sight."[69] When settlers learned that Bannock

Joe and several Indian women were being hidden by Albert Wilson in his barn at Emmettsville, a group of settlers rode out to investigate. The Indians were shot down when they tried to escape across the Payette River.[70]

General Howard was aware of the problems that scattered groups were causing, but the situation was now compounded. While his troops had pursued the Bannocks into eastern Idaho, military authorities at Fort Lapwai learned that a few of White Bird's Nez Perce and several Sioux had returned from exile in Canada and had been sighted on the Clearwater. This small group of Indians had "gone to the Salmon River to open caches and then join the Snakes." Howard ordered Colonel Wheaton to Fort Walla Walla, but directed him to leave Captain W. F. Drum with his hundred men in the upper Weiser country, with instructions to capture any Indians in the area and "quiet the apprehensions of the people."[71]

Even with Colonel Forsyth in command at Fort Boise and other troops vigorously pursuing the Indians across southern and eastern Idaho, many Indians managed to reach the Lemhi and Fort Hall reservations and eluded capture by mixing with Indians friendly to whites. By late August reports were coming in of battles and skirmishes with Bannock parties as far away as Montana and Wyoming. Reports of the capture of Bannock camps were widespread, but the Weisers proved to be more elusive. On August 25, 1878, "three Weiser Indians were captured" in the Pahsimeroi Valley when one of their camps was taken by surprise. Other camps had escaped. The three captives were brought to Fort Boise to be held with the other prisoners taken near Birch Creek.[72]

Following operations under Captain Drum (no first name recorded) in the upper Weiser and Payette country, peaceful conditions were reported from Salubria by the third week in August. While volunteer scouts announced occasional sightings of small Indian parties, the people felt safe enough to return to their homes. There was one Indian raid for horses on one of the ranches but the settlers themselves had gone in pursuit.[73]

This raid occurred on August 17, 1878, at William Munday's ranch. Munday, Jake Grosclose, Tom Healey, and "Three-Fingered" Smith tracked the Indians westward over the divide into Payette Valley. At the falls of the Payette (Cascade Falls), the men rode into an ambush, and at first fire Munday fell dead. Grosclose was struck and killed while he and Healy sought cover. Smith, "being a man experienced in such matters," was wounded, but escaped. He rode to Cal White's mail station at Salmon Meadows, where he reported that the massacre had been perpetrated by "at least 75 Indians."[74] Though renegade Indians were thought to be responsible for the attack, the Weisers were blamed, when Smith noted that "he distinguished the sound of Andy Johnson's rifle in that terrible affair."[75]

Captain Drum's command was at the head of the Weiser River and pursued the attackers. At Cascade Falls, he found and buried the three men and followed the Indian trail eight miles to Pearsall's Diggins, where he found the bodies of Daniel Crooks and Brady Wilhelm, two prospectors. The size of the raiding party had been exaggerated and was estimated at "not more than 15 bucks."[76] Captain Drum, after examining the area, felt that even this number was too high and reported that only "five had committed the murders." When Drum's reports of the ambush reached General Howard at Walla Walla, the general had his doubts about who was responsible for the tragedy, and was more "inclined to believe" that the "Nez Perce Indians from White Bird's band" were responsible.[77]

In the meantime, Sarah Winnemucca came to Fort Boise to interview captives who had been taken in other skirmishes. The Indian women refused to tell her anything, and when she tried to talk with the men, one of the women intervened and warned the men "to say nothing, as Sarah would be certain to tell everything they said to the officers." The only thing Sarah Winnemucca learned for sure was that the prisoners were not her Paiute people, but probably "Shoshones or Weisers." Sarah was later presented with letters of commendation by the military for her assistance during the "campaign against the Bannock, Piute, and Weiser Indians" that summer.[78]

Borland's Weiser volunteers joined Drum on the Payette, and scouting parties were sent out from a base camp to locate and overtake the small groups of Indians infiltrating the country. In the first week of September, the militia located a camp on the Gold Fork of the Payette, but the five Indians escaped on foot,

Sarah Winnemucca. (Courtesy of Nevada Historical Society)

losing their horses and supplies to the whites. Borland reported that he believed the camp had been occupied by the "Sheepeater Indians who have been intermarried with the Weisers," and he had little confidence of catching them before winter. He noted that one Indian "well known in that section" was Andy Johnson. This Indian leader was now believed to be at the head of the band and was known to have a Weiser wife, he said.[79]

Captain Drum kept his command in the upper Payette country through the month of September. By September 21, his patrols and scouting parties had searched, without results, Long Valley north to the Payette Lakes and had crossed over the mountains to the east onto the South Fork of the Salmon River. His field dispatches related that the "hostile Weisers" had left the area and taken refuge in the mountains. Their trails indicated that fifty were regrouping on the South Fork, forty-five miles south of Warrens. With rations running low, Drum was forced to abandon chase and return north to Camp Howard.[80]

Reports of small bands of hostiles continued to arrive at the capital during Drum's operation on the upper Payette. Renegade Indians were said to be in the vicinity of Yankee Fork and Cape Horn, where hostiles had attacked a party of packers. Another report came in of a skirmish on Squaw Creek, northwest of Emmettsville, with two Indians being "made good." Others were believed to be in the mountains between Squaw Creek and the Payette River. When the troops withdrew, the settlers felt vulnerable to attack by the Weisers and Bannocks, prompting government officials at Boise to request that troops be permanently stationed in Indian Valley. General Howard responded that he was unable to station troops there, but that he had ordered the troops at Fort Boise and Camp Howard to capture the few Indians still in the area.[81]

By the last of September, the pursuit of hostiles had ended and the Bannock War was officially over. The war had been costly. Nine soldiers and thirty-one citizens had been killed and eighteen others seriously wounded. Seventy-eight Indians had been reported killed and sixty-six others wounded; there were probably three times that many Indian casualties.[82] Government expenditures amounted to more than half a million dollars.

The personal cost to the Weisers had been devastating. Any type of "band" organization and unity had been shattered. Those who had not been killed or captured were reduced to small groups of fugitives hiding in the wilderness. Many had been forced to abandon their property and personal possessions during their hasty retreat from Oregon and were living in destitute condition in camps scattered from the Seven Devils Mountains to the Salmon River country of central Idaho.

Speculation over the causes of the uprising elicited many differing opinions in 1878. While the Bannocks appeared to have been justified in making war, little regard was given to the grievances of their Weiser and Paiute allies until years later. General Crook, commanding the Department of the Platte and a veteran of the Snake Wars of the 1860s, wrote that the Indian policy "has resolved itself into a question of Warpath or starvation; and, being merely human, many will choose the former alternative where death shall at least be glorious." In rebuttal to the "tenderhearted Indian fighter," the editor of the *Statesman* pointed out that "it was not the want of food which started them on the warpath, but their savage thirst for blood."[83] Agent Rhinehart was later to point out that

> after all, savages as they were, who can have the heart to blame them for fighting for their homes and the lives of their people? . . . I cannot say I know them . . . although they joined the Bannocks in 1878 and were nearly all exterminated, they left our handful of whites unmolested at the Agency. They went against General Howard's troops when they might have slain us and taken all the government stores. Despite their savagery in war, there is a deep tinge of pathos pervading the history and decline of the Indian race.[84]

SEVEN

A Final Resistance

THE SHEEPEATER CAMPAIGN

The end of the Bannock War and the noticeable withdrawal of troops at the beginning of winter in 1878 brought relief to the Weisers holding out in the mountains. They had no way of knowing, however, that by the end of October 1878, the military had abandoned pursuit, announced victory, and quit the war. As far as the whites were concerned the Bannock War was over, but many of the Weisers were being held in confinement at Fort Boise and were still classified as hostile fugitives.

In the middle of October, within weeks of Captain Drum's recall from the area, Indians stole fourteen head of horses from Indian Valley. A small party of whites tracked the "red murdering robbers" over the same route the participants of the Cascade Falls ambush had followed in August. Suspecting another trap at the falls, the whites turned back, convinced that the "Weiser Indians have not yet ceased hostilities and have no intention of soon doing so."[1]

Major John Green returned from an expedition to eastern Idaho and assumed the duties of commander at Fort Boise in the middle of September. By late October he was receiving reports that small groups of hostile Indians were camped near Yankee Fork and Cape Horn.[2] At least one group of Weisers, thought to be Eagle Eye's group, were located in the Seven Devils Mountains, northwest of Indian Valley. Others had made it to the safety of the deep canyons of the Salmon River country and had joined with the few Sheepeater families still living there. However, their hostilities ceased throughout the mountains.

The scattered Weisers and their Bannock allies were destitute. They had lost their possessions and winter food supplies, and must have spent a miserable winter in the mountains. With the tragedy of the Bannock War and the dreams of reclaiming their homeland shattered, the object now became one of survival.

For a short time following the Bannock War at least three Weiser families escaped detection and remained in the immediate region of their homelands: Eagle Eye's extended family, the destitute Sheepeater family of Andy Johnson, and the families of the Nez Perce headman, Indian Charley, and his son.

By spring 1879, word arrived in the white settlements of yet another incident when five Chinese miners were killed on Loon Creek, a tributary of the Middle Fork of the Salmon River, about one hundred miles northeast of Boise.[3] The Sheepeaters were suspect, even though the murders may have been committed by a party of white men disguised as Indians, according to a rumor that was "noised around in Bonanza."[4]

In May, two white settlers, Hugh Johnson and Peter Dorsey, were found dead on the South Fork of the Salmon and "the circumstances warranted the conclusion that the outrages had been committed by Redskins."[5] Army troops who later investigated the scene, however, concluded "that it was very convenient to have some Indians in one's neighborhood in case of a crime being committed. It gives one a chance to shift the blame on the Indians."[6] But, as was often the case in the "violence prone, well armed mining camps," the atrocities were blamed on the Indians.[7] It was well known in military circles that a few of the whites were "anxious for another Indian War in the Boise Country" because of the financial benefits to be gained in the path of a military campaign, as was the case in the Nez Perce War in 1877 and the Bannock War of 1878.[8]

The death of the five Chinese and the two whites could not be overlooked. On May 1, 1879, Major General Irvin McDowell, commander of the Military Department of the Columbia, directed General Howard to send a detachment to Loon Creek to investigate the murder of the Chinese miners, rumored to have been committed by "some of the hostiles of last summer, who have been wintering with the Sheepeaters on the Middle Fork of the Salmon."[9] Howard was one step ahead of his commander and had already completed a plan for a campaign against the Indians, confirming that he was satisfied that there was "a party of last years hostiles on the Middle Fork of the Salmon."[10] The approval on May 3 of Howard's plan signalled the beginning of the Sheepeater Campaign and the last of Idaho's Indian wars.[11]

While some of the Weiser holdouts followed War Jack into the Sheepeater troubles of 1879, others did not. The families of Eagle Eye and Indian Charley stayed clear of the army campaign directed at the Sheepeater stronghold on the Middle Fork of the Salmon River by remaining secluded in isolated niches in the mountains.

The Sheepeaters on the Middle Fork, together with the few Weisers and Bannocks taking refuge there, were doubted to number "more than one hundred and fifty, all told," but were known to be able to endure great hardship and exist for days on meager rations. In addition, they were also known to be "familiar with every gorge, defile and trail" in the area.[12] The country was unexplored and was among the roughest and most isolated mountain ranges of any in the Northwest.

On May 31, 1879, Captain Bernard left Fort Boise for Challis and Loon Creek with a cavalry company of 56 plus Robbins's scouts. Another company of mounted infantry, under Lieutenant Henry Catley, left Camp Howard, near Grangeville, for Warrens. A third force of twenty Umatilla Indian scouts was organized by Lieutenants E. S. Farrow and W. C. Brown, who, with seven enlisted men and four packers, departed the Umatilla agency on July 7 for the Weiser country.

It had been a late spring, and the campaign was difficult. Catley reached Warrens by a series of forced marches, but reported on July 11 that he was unable to proceed due to snow. A month later he was only as far as the mouth of the South Fork of the Salmon. Bernard's forces fared little better in their attempt to reach the Middle Fork from Cape Horn. In early July they reported that "a trail through timber and rocks had to be made all the way" to enable them to reach the river. On July 15 Bernard wrote Howard that "the country is no doubt as rough as any in the United States, and to get at the Indians will be a work of great difficulty."[13]

Farrow and his Indian scouts reached Brownlee Ferry, crossed into Idaho Territory, passed through Indian Valley, and made their way to Cal White's Mail Station at Salmon Meadows,

Lieutenant Edward S. Farrow. (Courtesy of Idaho State Historical Society)

near the headwaters of the Weiser River. White reported that even though no Indians had been sighted, smoke and signal fires had been sighted on surrounding mountains. He estimated that more than 150 Indians had established themselves at the mouth of the Secesh River near Warren.[14] Farrow sent his scouts into Council Valley, where, on July 16, he reported signs of Indians near Wood's Creek, but after scouting the country he was unable to locate them. On July 27 his scouts found more signs, soon discovering a camp and a herd of animals. He immediately sent word to Bernard's command and discovered the next day that the camp belonged to white men, purporting to be miners, with bands of horses. Bernard's command had marched seventy miles out of their way.[15]

In the meantime, Catley crossed over the mountains onto Big Creek, a tributary of the Middle Fork of the Salmon. On July 29, after signs of Indians on the twenty-eighth, they continued down Big Creek and destroyed an Indian camp that had been abandoned only two hours before they arrived. They followed the Indian trail down the creek into a steep canyon, where about a dozen Indians were waiting in ambush. The Indians routed Catley and his force of seventy men. Two of his men were wounded, so Catley stopped the retreat only a few miles up the creek and made camp for the night. Catley thought to continue the retreat the next day.[16]

The next morning he moved the command up the side of a hill in an attempt to escape the canyon, but was held back from high points by Indian snipers. Other Indians set fire to the base of the mountain, and the winds carried the fire uphill toward the soldiers. The wind shifted in time, and a group of soldiers set backfires. That night, under the cover of darkness, Catley abandoned most of the baggage and supplies and retreated toward Warren with the intention of going back to Camp Howard.[17]

War Jack and his small Indian force pursued the soldiers out of Big Creek and down onto the South Fork, to within a few miles of Warren. Coming upon an isolated ranch, they attacked, as a "legitimate sequel to Catley's defeat," killing owner James Rains and wounding another man named Albert Webber before returning to the Sheepeater stronghold. Two whites hiding in a nearby field escaped and carried the news of the attack back to the mining camp.[18]

When news of Catley's disaster reached General Howard, he was shocked by the lieutenant's apparent misconduct and noted to Bernard, then near the Payette Lakes, that "retreat before inferior numbers" was astounding. A troop of twenty-five men under Captain A. G. Forse was immediately dispatched from Camp Howard to "turn the command toward and not from this small body of Indians."[19]

All military forces converged on Big Creek. Farrow's scouts arrived first and took up pursuit into the Middle Fork. Bernard, reinforced by Catley and Forse, followed close behind. Signs of Indians were everywhere. The military troops passed abandoned wickiups and fish traps, and on August 19, the scouts had a brief skirmish with a group of Indians. Catley found a camp of ten wickiups and abandoned supplies together with other Indians belongings, but the Indians had escaped into the hills, setting fire to the forest behind them to discourage pursuit.[20]

The following day Indian snipers fired on a pack train and killed trooper Harry Egan. He was the only soldier killed during the campaign. With the Indians now reduced to eating mules,[21] Farrow followed them down the Middle Fork and soon reported that the Indians were "in full retreat, abandoning property all along the trail."[22] Captain Bernard instructed him to keep after them as long as his rations held out, noting that "the hostiles do not exceed 30 warriors" and appeared to be going toward the Lemhi country. Bernard took the remainder of the command and headed toward Loon Creek to meet the supply train. He reported that most of the horses were exhausted, and without rest and forage all would soon give out.[23]

When General Howard received reports of the condition of the troops and mounts, he authorized Bernard to return to Boise and recalled the other troops to their posts. "The expedition has not accomplished what was expected by myself, or demanded by your instructions," he reported to McDowell. "Lieutenant Catley appears to be much to blame for his timid action and hasty retreat for more than 100 miles. He will be given an opportunity to make full explanation."[24]

Bernard's arrival in Boise, apparently without success, agitated the editor of the *Statesman*. In an editorial he suggested that a "reward of $500 per head would probably be the cheapest way of closing them out. . . . These Indians are enemies to mankind, and have no more right to live than Guerrilla highway men. To shoot them down would be an act of justice to the human family."[25]

Lieutenants Farrow and Brown had decided to make one more attempt against the Sheepeaters before leaving the area. On September 17, the small force of scouts left Rains's ranch on the South Fork and once again followed Catley's original trail into the rugged Middle Fork. At noon the next day, they surprised and captured two Indian women with a child, and two young boys, though one of the boys soon escaped. Several hunting camps were also discovered, a short distance away, but the Indians had fled, leaving behind their provisions and a few horses.[26]

For nearly a week the scouts combed the Sheepeater country and uncovered several other abandoned Indian camps. Using what information they were able to obtain from the two captive women, they attempted to contact the elusive Sheepeaters. On September 25, their camp was hailed by a lone warrior from the timber, and Brown and one of the Umatillas, Wa-tis-kow-kow, met him and asked him into camp for a parley. The warrior said he was War Jack, "successor to Eagle Eye," and told them he was tired of fighting and wanted to quit. After he agreed to an unconditional surrender, he was sent out to bring in the other members of the Sheepeater force.[27]

The next day he returned with "a Weiser named Bouyer," whose family turned out to be the captives taken a week before. The Indians were scattered through the area in small groups, with Bouyer, War Jack, and a Lemhi named Chuck as the principal leaders. Bouyer and War Jack were sent out to bring in those they could induce to come. On October 1, War Jack returned with another Weiser at the head of "four lodges, consisting of eight men and twenty-four squaws and papooses (nearly all Sheepeaters) and doing justice to the occasion by liberal use of feathers and paint."[28] Later surrenders increased this total to fifty-one, of whom only fifteen could be classified as warriors. The demoralized and destitute prisoners admitted to attacking Rains's ranch following Catley's invasion of the Middle Fork, but they denied any responsibility for the massacre on Loon Creek.

General Howard was happy to report, on October 9, that the campaign's failure was now "reversed, and the expedition

Charlie Shaplish, or Whirlwind (left), and Wa-tis-kow-kow (right), Umatilla scouts. (Courtesy of Idaho State Historical Society)

has handsomely been completed by Lieutenant Farrow and his scouts, having defeated the Indians in two skirmishes'' and captured their camps and provisions. Reporting that ''the entire band'' had surrendered and were en route to Vancouver as ''prisoners of war,'' the Sheepeater Campaign was officially brought to an end. The Indian prisoners, with War Jack as their headman, numbered twenty-three Salmon River Sheepeaters, thirteen Weisers, and seven Boise Indians in their group in March 1881, just prior to their transfer from Vancouver to Fort Hall.[29]

As an epilogue to the campaign, Sven Liljeblad summed it up best:

> The armament of this formidable foe, pursued for three months by the United States cavalry, mounted infantry, and enlisted Umatilla scouts, totaled four carbines, one breech-loading and two muzzle-loading rifles, and one double-barrelled shotgun. This

pathetic affair is committed to memory by Idaho historians under the presumptuous title of "the Sheepeater War."[30]

A LAST SANCTUARY

Howard's optimistic report that the "entire Sheepeater" had been brought in at the end of 1879 was proved false, and many whites contended that less than half of the Indians had surrendered. While the scattered Middle Fork Indians were being taken, reports of other groups continued to arrive at Boise. Horses were run off in Indian Valley and there was trouble on Squaw Creek, near Horseshoe Bend, when a white youth was wounded in an encounter with a band of "mixed Bannock and Weisers," numbering from forty to sixty individuals.[31]

In response, Farrow instructed Brown to delay the command at Indian and Council Valleys, scout the country for stolen stock, and locate any Indians or horse thieves in the area.[32] After nearly a week of battling deep snows and winter weather, Brown was forced to call off the expedition and return to the Umatilla Agency.

In spring of 1880, there were renewed reports of sightings around Indian Valley and rumors of a possible encampment of Weisers at the mouth of Crooked River. A volunteer force of whites encountered an Indian picketing his horse and were fired on by a band of "ten or fifteen Indians" when they approached. Two whites were wounded. White trackers trailed two of the Indians over the mountains into Long Valley before "prudential reasons" caused them to turn back.[33]

In early summer a settler at Indian Valley captured two Indian women in the mountains above the settlement. The women identified themselves as "the daughters of Eagle Eye" and, within a day or two, another party was sighted on Cottonwood, six miles above the valley. The two captives were held prisoner while whites sent for troops from Boise."[34]

It was no surprise that there were still Weisers in the mountains. Military authorities had already learned, through the Sheepeater captives at Vancouver, that there were "still others of their kind in the region known as the Upper Salmon River country."[35] Lieutenant P. S. Bomus, from Boise, was dispatched with a detachment of troops to Indian Valley, but the Weisers escaped into the mountains and he soon returned. The two captured women were placed with the other Indian prisoners held at Fort Boise since the end of the Bannock War.[36]

Farrow was again called to the field and his command spent the rest of the summer in a futile attempt to locate and bring in the rest of the Weisers. Andy Johnson, Big John, and Old Chuck were unaccounted for, although one story circulated that Chuck had been killed on the upper Payette in the fall of 1878. By August, Farrow was reported to be in pursuit of the Indians once again and had sent word for a supply train to meet him on the Payette River at Packer John Mountain, not far from Garden Valley. By early October, he was still in pursuit and had scouted the Crooked River country, Long Valley, and the South Fork of the Salmon. The Indians eluded his force even though War Jack was now employed by the government as one of his scouts. The scouts found a small party estimated at forty or fifty Indians on the Middle Fork of the Salmon, but Farrow was ordered to return and disband his unit before he had taken action.[37]

Reports continued to arrive at the capital in the fall and early winter of 1880. Miners on Squaw Creek reported an encounter with a group of twenty Indians, who threatened the whites with death if they told the soldiers of their location.[38] But the Indians were worn out and destitute. With their organized resistance broken, and scattered families unable to reorganize, several groups went into hiding. Others drifted eastward to the safety of the reservations at Lemhi and Fort Hall.

By the spring of 1881, reports of Indians in the Weiser area had all but ceased. A long report reached Boise that a miner from Warren had spotted several Indian boys in Long Valley attempting to catch birds on the Payette. A group of whites quickly organized on the Little Salmon and went to the scene only to find that the Indians had left the area, following the trail over the divide toward Indian Valley.[39] They left behind the evidence of the desperate conditions to which they had been reduced:

> Their intentions were evidently friendly. The party appeared to consist of three bucks, two squaws, two boys and a child. A visit to their camp indicated that they were entirely destitute of ammunition. They had peeled bark from a great many trees, and had been scraping and apparently living on the soft portions of it, but

> there was not a bone or feather to be found, although game was plenty thereabouts. They are supposed to be a well known Indian named Andy Johnson, whose whereabout had not been satisfactorily accounted for, who with his family and friends are seeking the white settlement through starvation.[40]

Following the report, a company of cavalry under Captain W. P. Parnell was dispatched from Boise "to scout into the Payette Lake region" during the summer of 1881.[41] If any of the Weisers still remained in the area, Parnell failed to find them and the soldiers returned to the fort empty-handed. The surviving members of Eagle Eye's clan had disappeared without a trace, and for a time, they and their leader were lost to history.

The Indians in the mountains including Weisers, Bannocks, and Middle Fork Sheepeaters had three options open to them: continue to hold out in the wilderness, surrender to the authorities and join those held prisoners, or attempt to reach a reservation and submit to an unknown fate. Returning to the Malheur Reservation was out of the question. That reservation was never reactivated; following the Bannock War, whites illegally took over those agency lands. Agent Rinehart and General Howard recommended that the agency be abandoned, and their suggestion was being followed. The Indian prisoners held there had been sent to Yakima and other agencies.[42]

The Weisers, led by Indian Charley, decided to seek safety somewhere in the region of their mountains. In spite of the fact that the old peace leader and his son had both been blinded in one eye for refusing to fight the whites in an earlier war, several of the Shoshoni men had continued to follow him.[43]

Eventually, Indian Charley found an ideal hiding spot south of Long Valley on the banks of the Payette River and near the site of one of their summer camps. "As far back as their memories reached, the valley from the bend of the river to Payette Lake had been their summer range where they had gathered food, fished, and hunted deer."[44]

Eagle Eye and the remaining members of his immediate family joined them there, choosing the mountains high above Indian Charley's river location as a safer haven. They located in the Dry Buck Valley, south of High Valley and in the vicinity of Timber Butte, sometime prior to 1888.

Located to the west, between the deep canyon of the Payette River and Squaw Creek, the Dry Buck area proved to be an ideal sanctuary. The trails from the north bypassed the high mountain valley and rugged river canyon, with the main trail branching north of their location. At Round Valley, the trail to Boise Basin crossed over Packer John Mountain and into Garden Valley, located to the east. The other trail crossed the river at Smith's Ferry and passed down the Squaw Creek drainage to the west, en route to Emmettsville, Horseshoe Bend, and Boise City.[45] They were hidden away in their wilderness, and for the first time in years, they were able to reorganize and take stock of their situation.

With the end of the Indian Wars in Idaho and the disappearance of the Indians in the area, stories of hostile Indians on the warpath and depredations in western Idaho Territory came to an end. The Malheur Reservation was closed by executive order on May 21, 1883,[46] and the Indian prisoners being held at Boise and other military posts were eventually returned to their tribal reservations, with most of the Weiser survivors being sent to join other Shoshoni at Fort Hall.

The Indians at Fort Hall continued to visit the Weiser country during the summers, though in smaller numbers, to hunt and fish in the high country, but the settlers were not threatened. The Indian Wars curtailed the annual migrations after food for most of the Shoshoni, but small groups of Indians still visited the Weiser area until at least after the turn of the century.[47] Remarked one early resident:

> They rode ponies single file and usually camped for a night or two at the end of town. This caused a lot of excitement. We kids enjoyed going down to visit with them. The Indians were usually friendly and seemed pleased to have us visit them. They let us know they were on their way to Payette Lakes where they would catch whitefish and salmon to salt down, dry, smoke and then pack for winter use. Huckleberries were plentiful and hunting good, so when they returned in the fall, they were well supplied for the winter months.[48]

The Payette area provided not only a safe haven for the Weisers, but also good hunting and fishing, and they settled into an existence free of hostile whites. Occasionally, they joined their

Sheepeater relatives who had been captured on the Middle Fork and spent time with them at the fishery on the Payette Lakes.[49]

As for Andy Johnson, there is every indication that he and his family eventually reached the white settlements on the Weiser. Apparently he was met by sympathetic settlers and former white friends. It is generally accepted that his family settled down on the Weiser, at least until the middle 1880s, and that several of his five children attended the school before eventually going onto the reservation.[50]

Rumors and stories along the lower Payette River from Horseshoe Bend to Emmett during the 1880s circulated the legend of a ''One-Eyed Tribe.'' However, it was too soon after the Indian troubles for the whites to approach or become friendly with the small group of Indians.[51]

Indian Charley's family group soon found out that they were not to be alone even in this forgotten part of Idaho. Jimmy Hoy (also spelled Hay, Hoey), an Irish trapper and mountain man, built cabins there with a friend on a flat near the mouth of Dry Buck Creek, a mile below the confluence of the forks of the Payette River. Here they met and ''were joined by a band of about thirty Indians''[52] and soon became good friends with the Weiser people. Hoy eventually married one of the Indian women and settled there permanently.

The arrival of several white families in the vicinity convinced the Indian settlers that their era had passed. They felt they had to align themselves with the white man and make concessions to the white style of living if they were to survive, and they realized that by accepting the white man's way of life, advantages might be gained for their people.

''Entirely on their own and without being prodded by a government agent, they soon became fully familiar with this new mode of life'' and located small homesteads in the area. The native settlers learned to build log cabins and frame houses for permanent shelter. They planted and cultivated crops, kept pigs and chickens, and ''took a particular pride in planting fruit trees.''[53]

The Indian families were soon self-sufficient and produced virtually all of their own necessities. Many of the wild crops on which they were dependent grew in the area, and they continued to gather them to supplement the vegetables grown in their fields

Takuarikas, a Sheepeater woman captured during the campaign of 1878 and taken to Fort Hall, photographed at McCall, Idaho, around the turn of the century. She and her relatives often returned to hunt and fish at the Payette Lakes with the Weiser Indians. (Courtesy of Idaho State Historical Society)

and gardens. They made their own teas of mint and broth and rarely purchased luxury items such as coffee, sugar, and flour.[54] Hunting and fishing remained an important function—the surrounding area was rich in wild game—but they no longer depended on it. By supplementing their diet with deer, elk, and salmon, they were able to build up herds of cattle and horses, and they grew enough wheat to supply themselves with flour.[55]

No record exists of a time of hunger or starvation after the Weisers settled. The opposite appears to have been the case. The Indians were expert at preparing dried fruits, vegetables, smoked meats and fish. During hard times all the Weisers would travel to wherever food was plentiful, and family groups would share and help each other.[56]

By 1888, word of the Indian colony had reached the white settlements. Eagle Eye's venture at the Dry Buck community received favorable response in Boise, presumably because his actual identity was unknown. The *Statesman* picked up the story:

> In Dry Buck Valley, between upper Squaw Creek and High Valley in Boise County, in this territory, live the last relics of several different tribes of aborigines of the once famous tribes of Idaho. There are seventeen women and children and three bucks. One of the latter claims to be the age of Methuselah. . . . They came from no man knows where and were occupants of that valley for some time before the nearest white settler knew of their presence. Only of late has the inborn hatred of the red man for the white been overcome. They are employed by the sawmill company in that vicinity in gently tilting the monster sawlogs cut at the mill.[57]

The Weiser settlers learned that some risk had to be taken to trust whites, and by necessity they abandoned their shy existence. Some of them got jobs at the sawmills at Dry Buck and on Soldier Creek. White families in Emmettsville made friends with them and contributed to their material comfort. In time, the Indian men managed to get occasional work in the hay fields at Jerusalem, a few miles down river and north of Horseshoe Bend, while the women produced leather and beadwork for extra income.[58]

It is curious to note that while these Weiser families were succeeding in the white world, the opposite was true for the reservation Indians at Lemhi and Fort Hall. They were being pushed by the authorities and agents into white civilization, and most of them resisted. "All they want," reported the Fort Hall agent in 1890, "is enough to eat, with as little exertion on their part as possible." Noting that many were "shiftless, careless, wasteful, and extravagant," there was a lack of interest in farming at the agency. By 1893, only 130 families had engaged themselves in any form of agriculture.[59]

The process of acculturation, of forceful conversion, was an even bigger failure with Chief Tendoy's people at the small Lemhi Reservation. "It is clear in my mind," wrote the agent there, "that these Indians will never be a progressive people until the tribal religions and customs which are firmly held intact by the Chief are broken." And until that time, "they will never exercise the individual thought and action necessary to become successful farmers."[60]

One Idaho historian noted that the weakness of the Indian policy could be characterized by saying that the reservation Indians were likened to a "corralled ox" and that the government had crushed from them all semblance of independence.[61] But from the Indian standpoint, their situation was probably better expressed by the Sioux chief Sitting Bull when he said: "God Almighty made me an Indian, and he did not make me an agency Indian, and I do not intend to be one."

THE FINAL YEARS

In 1890, Idaho Territory became a state. Progress spread rapidly into the Weiser homeland. The lands around the Weiser colony on the Payette River were surveyed in May 1892, and the surveyor noted in his report the "good log houses" belonging to the Indians, as well as the gardens and fields in the area.[62]

As early as 1880, General Howard had pointed out that Indians were frequently being displaced by whites, "who know just how to take up the land in a legal way." Already the country north of Emmett was becoming an important range for sheep and cattle, and by 1894, over 1,500 head of sheep and cattle had been driven into the high country by white ranchers. To protect their land rights, the Indian group filed on their homesteads, becoming "the only case of its kind in the state."[63]

The filing of homesteads by other Indians through the United States created a stir in some white circles. Many whites opposed such a move. Letters of protest were written to public officials, prompting D. M. Browning, Commissioner of Indian Affairs, to point out in 1895, that whites "seem to have very little respect for the rights of Indians who have segregated themselves from their tribes and sought to avail themselves of the benefits of the Indian homestead and allotment laws enacted expressly for them by Congress." He noted that Indians, in general, had been encouraged to "abandon their old habits, adopt the pursuits of civilized life, and invited to take homes on the public domain," and furthermore, his office was duty bound to protect those rights.[64]

Browning had to point out that helping Indians combat the "greedy spirit of the white man" was difficult because many Indian homesteads were remote. The agents had to travel long distances, at great expense, to assist them, and often found that they were away hunting or working. Communication by mail was also difficult; many had no addresses or were not known to the post office, which they seldom, if ever, visited.[65]

By 1896, the legal contests of Indian rights to occupy public lands under the same conditions as whites continued to build, not only in Idaho, but throughout the West. The commissioner reported that the lands of the Indian homesteaders appeared to have "a pecular attraction for a certain class of white men. They seek the home of an Indian because they apprehend that the land contains valuable minerals, water facilities, timber, or a soil better adapted to the purposes of agriculture or grazing than other portions of the surrounding country."[66]

Eagle Eye and his family, like Indian Charley on the river, continued to improve their homesteads near Timber Butte. As the memories of the Indian wars faded, racial tensions eased.

"About three miles below the sawmill," wrote a white friend who spent her summers at the Joe Reed's Mountain Lumber Company in the high country, "there are quite a number of Indians. They are renegades from other tribes, but are now civilized and perfectly harmless."[67]

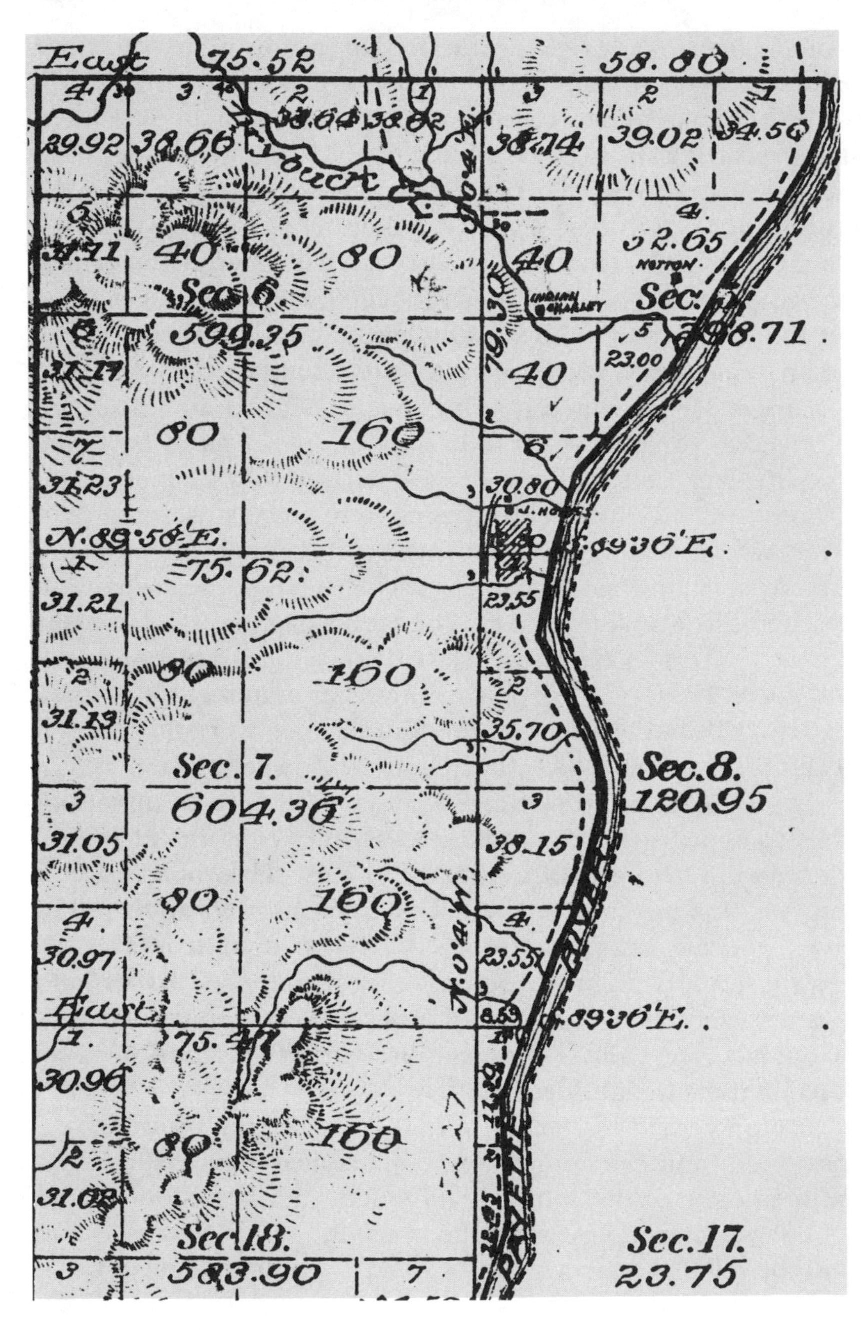

Dry Buck Valley Survey Map, 1892.
(Courtesy of Idaho State Historical Society)

It is not certain when Eagle Eye moved down out of the high Dry Buck Valley onto the lower slopes of Timber Butte, but it is likely that his white friends at the sawmills and in the local mines influenced him. Further, it is probable that outside of the Indians themselves, only this select nucleus of trusted whites actually knew the real identity of the old Shoshoni headman, and they did not break this trust openly until after his death.

As the end of the century approached, tragic events marked a turning point for the Indian colonies at both Timber Butte and on the Payette. The first tragedy followed a placer mining accident at Dry Buck near the end of May 1896:[68]

''Eagle Eye, the Chief of the Dry Buck Indians is dead,'' came word from Reed's sawmill, and the writer noted that the old headman's people were languishing. ''He was the leader of the band who killed Monday [*sic*], Haley [*sic*], and Goosco [sic] in Long Valley about 16 years ago.''[69]

Mourning the loss of the Shoshoni leader, the Indian families gathered together to carry the old headman and warrior to the top of Timber Butte. There, they laid him to rest overlooking the Squaw Creek Valley, in sight of the mountains of his homeland on the Weiser.[70]

The following year the foundations of the community were shaken again—this time on the river. On Sunday, June 20, 1897, the aged mountaineer, James Hoy, passed away. That winter, before the year was up, devastation struck the Indian settlement still a third time with the death of Indian Charley, the Nez Perce headman.[71] Thus, within a period of two years, the Weiser colonists witnessed the passing of a warrior generation and the last of the old-line traditional leaders.

Eagle Eye's sons remained at the core of the group[72] although it appears that Young Charley, Indian Charley's son, became the leader of the native settlers. George F. Cook of Sweet, a white miner who had a claim near the Weiser homesteads and for whom the Indians sometimes worked, looked after their interests and continued to help the Indian settlement stay on a self-supporting basis. In spite of the loss of Hoy and the old headmen, the Indians were determined and continued to occupy and improve their homesteads, less than a section altogether, and Young Charley formally entered their lands for patent.[73]

By 1898, Idaho Senator George L. Shoup had received enough complaints from disgruntled whites to draw his attention to the group on the Payette. Compounding this situation was the discovery of another group of "Weiser" Indians living near Camas Prairie, in the vicinity of the white settlement at Bliss, Idaho. A few of the white settlers there were complaining of their presence and wanted them removed to Fort Hall. In February, Shoup sent a letter to the Commissioner of Indian Affairs requesting that an inspector be sent to influence the two "destitute" Indian groups to go to the reservation where they could get proper attention.[74]

Indian Inspector William McConnell, ex-governor and former leader of the Payette vigilante group during the 1860s, went to visit the Weisers along the Payette in April, and was well received by Young Charley and his people. His report received favorable coverage in the *Statesman*:

> It appears there are 20 Indians living at that point. They have been there 12 or 14 years. Two of them are Snake River Indians and the rest are supposed to be Nez Perces. Just why they located at that isolated point is not known. The Indians themselves will not explain the matter, but the supposition is that their settling there was a result of some feud. . . . The Indians cultivate their property, raising grain and other crops. They have set out fruit trees, and they have considerable stock, including horses, cattle, and chickens. Mr. McConnell says he will ask the government to purchase for them a small tract in the canyon that they failed to secure. They are better off there, he says, than they would be if they were with the tribe, being the most comfortable fixed band of Indians that he knows of.[75]

In June 1898, Fort Hall's new agent, C. A. Warner, visited and met with two headmen, Old Tom and Captain Jack. He reported that they "had a great many horses, and by hunting, fishing, and root digging live pretty well." The Indians resisted going to the reservation because of the lack of food and poor hunting and, as they put it, it was "two days eat, five days no eat."[76] Attempts to remove them were dropped when white settlers gave their support and asked that the Indians be allowed to stay. The Camas Prairie group was allowed to remain off the reservation and were officially carried on the Indian rolls as the "band of Camas Jim" until 1899.[77]

The Weiser colony on the Payette continued to flourish for several years following the losses of their leaders and were the last of Idaho's Indians to submit to reservation life. " 'Civilized' though they had become, they were no more acceptable to their Euroamerican neighbors, who coveted the Indian farms than the acculturated Cherokees had been to their Georgia neighbors."[78] In the face of government coercion and the "constant pressure on them from the white homesteaders in the valley," they had continued to occupy their farms.[79]

But, reluctantly, and for reasons unknown, the Indian families finally gave in. Some of Eagle Eye's group decided to move to the Lemhi Reservation, where they still had relatives. "One day in early summer, sometime about the turn of the century," the group gathered together with what few belongings they could carry and left their Payette farms and the Weiser country forever. Avoiding the public roads and frequented trails, they spent the entire summer crossing the mountains to reach the Lemhi.[80] Others went to Challis, but wound up at Fort Hall.

"Although the loss these emigrants had suffered in having to give up their native ground and spontaneous enterprise must have been appalling to them all,"[81] they must have been further distressed at the culture shock awaiting them on reaching Tendoy's mixed band at Lemhi. The severe restrictions of the tiny reservation barely supported the Indian population already there and, although the reservation Indians led by Tendoy were still resisting efforts to get them to take up farming, there was little land suitable for such enterprises.[82]

For the progressive Weisers, their arrival at Lemhi must have been like stepping back into time, to that period over twenty years before, following the Indian wars. As late as 1898, the agent, E. M. Yearian, had reported that Tendoy's people were "far from being civilized" and "still adear to Age Old Customs" with "2/3 of males over 18 in native costume—moccasins, leggings, breechcloth, blanket, feathers and paint."[83]

For the acculturated younger generation of the Weiser colony, who had never known anything but the more conventional life on the Payette, the effects must have been stunning. Even for those who were older, it was difficult because they had been mere children during the Indian wars. More alarming than all this was the news that they would once again be forced to give up yet another home. A treaty signed by Tendoy in 1880 agreeing to give up the reservation had finally been ratified by the government on February 23, 1898. The entire Indian population was destined to be removed to Fort Hall. Many of the Lemhi Indians had already voluntarily taken that step. By 1905, the census showed that 288 Shoshonis, 97 Sheepeaters, and 81 Bannocks, totalling 466 Indians, were still on the Lemhi, down from a population of 512 counted five years before.[84]

Following Tendoy's death in 1907, Eagle Eye's Weisers moved with the Lemhi Indians to Fort Hall. They were all amalgamated into the Shoshoni-Bannock tribe. Some descendants of Eagle Eye live today on the Fort Hall Indian Reservation under the last name *Eagle*.[85] The Hoy, Thorpe, Calico, Teton, Blackhawk, Tistibo, Kaiyou and other Shoshoni families also have lineage descending from Weiser origins. Some of them, and their children in time, became citizens of great prestige in their new community.[86] Because the enterprising Weisers had learned property values, they were able to obtain land allotments through the Dawes Act and once again took up farming and a settled way of life. In time, some of them became successful ranchers on Lincoln Creek and elsewhere on the reservation.[87]

> One and only one of the Indians ever returned to the Payette. Jimmy Hoy, Jr., the half-breed natural son of the trapper and an Indian woman, came back to work in the Jerusalem hay fields for several years. He claimed his father's name, but had no legal rights, and the title to Jimmy's property went to Boise County. Tragically, the life of this native son of the Payette was taken by a white man's bullet in a saloon brawl at Horseshoe Bend, when the railroad progress and so-called civilization came to the Payette.[88]

EIGHT

Conclusion

In the late 1930s, due to a shift in policy at Washington, leaders of the Shoshoni nation petitioned the government to allow the Indians to file claims over their lost lands. In 1940, the Indians at Fort Hall asked Idaho Congressman Henry Dworshak to have the government consider the aboriginal land interests of the Weiser Shoshoni, at a time when the Shoshoni nation was preparing to present their case before the Indian Claims Commission.[1] Expert witnesses later testified that the Weiser Shoshoni could not claim "exclusive use and occupancy" because they had shared the area with the Northern Paiute and Nez Perce, therefore no separate claim was to be allowed.

In the summer of 1962, Mrs. Josephine Thorpe, a member of the former Payette colony and granddaughter of Eagle Eye, visited the long-forgotten sites occupied by the native families at Dry Buck and along the Payette River, an area now known as Banks, Idaho. In the company of Merle W. Wells of the Idaho State Historical Society, and Sven Liljeblad of Idaho State University, she took her family on a tour in the area where she had spent her early childhood. More than half a century had passed, but they found ancient apple trees, perhaps the only surviving relics of the homesteads that had belonged to her people. At Emmett, Mrs. Thorpe visited her old friends, the Parrish family, and talked with Ella Knox Parrish of the days spent at Dry Buck. She was to journey once again to the top of Timber Butte, there to stand beside her grandfather's grave for a final time.[2]

Because she wanted to leave a legacy for her people, Mrs. Thorpe, a dignified and elegant lady, dictated an intriguing narrative about what she remembered of Indian life on the Payette.[3] Shortly after this fascinating interview, both she and Birdie

Ancient apple trees near Timber Butte believed to be the only surviving relics of the Weiser colony. (Photo by author)

Calico, the last surviving members of the nonreservation Weiser Shoshoni, passed away.

Today, lineage and kindred identification has not been lost at the Fort Hall Indian Reservation, and the Weiser spirit and resolve, though many times shaken, has never broken. The descendants of Eagle Eye now flourish as a lasting and living monument to the vanished members of the original band.

NOTES

CHAPTER 1. INDIANS IN THE WEISER VALLEY

1. Sven Liljeblad, *The Idaho Indians in Transition, 1805–1960*, p. 8.
2. Cornelius J. Brosnan, *History of the State of Idaho*, p. 28.
3. F. Ross Peterson, *Idaho, A Bicentennial History*, p. 21; Merle W. Wells, Interview by author, Boise, Idaho, July 13, 1988; Omer C. Stewart, *Indians of the Great Basin*, p. 27.
4. Brigham D. Madsen, *Chief Pocatello, The "White Plume,"* p. 10; Brigham D. Madsen, *The Northern Shoshoni*, p. 18; Merle W. Wells, Interview by author, Boise, Idaho, July 17, 1988.
5. William Asworth, *Hells Canyon, The Deepest Gorge on Earth*, p. 6.
6. Deward E. Walker, Jr., *Indians of Idaho*, p. 99; Robert F. Murphy and Yolanda Murphy, "Shoshone-Bannock Subsistence and Society," *University of California Anthropological Records* 16 (7), p. 318.
7. Francis Haines, *Indians of the Great Basin and Plateau*, p. 34.
8. Max G. Pavesic, Interview by author, Boise, Idaho, September 23, 1985.
9. Murphy and Murphy, "Shoshone-Bannock Subsistence and Society," p. 318; Asworth, *Hells Canyon*, p. 6; Brigham D. Madsen, *The Bannock of Idaho*, p. 24; Alvin M. Josephy, Jr., *The Nez Perce Indians and the Opening of the Northwest*, p. 20; Merle W. Wells, Interview by author, Boise, Idaho, July 13, 1988; Sven Liljeblad, Letter to author, Boise, Idaho, April 28, 1988; Robert H. Lowie, "The Northern Shoshone," *Anthropological Papers of the American Museum of Natural History*, Vol. II, Part II, p. 172.
10. John R. Swanton, *Indian Tribes of North America*, p. 405; Madsen, *The Northern Shoshoni*, p. 18; Merle W. Wells, Interview by author, Boise, Idaho, July 13, 1988.
11. Liljeblad, *The Idaho Indians in Transition*, p. 18. Max G. Pavesic, Interview by author, Boise, Idaho, October 14, 1985; Jon P. Dayley, "An Ethno-Historical Shoshone Narrative, Pie Nimmin Naakkanna, 'How We Lived Long Ago,' " *Idaho Archaeologist*, p. 1; Murphy and Murphy, "Shoshone-Bannock Subsistence and Society," p. 318; Sven Liljeblad, Letter to author, July 17, 1988.
12. Brigham D. Madsen, *The Lembi: Sacajawea's People*, p. 25; Jack Harris, "The White Knife Shoshoni of Nevada," *Acculturation in Seven American Indian Tribes*; Julian H. Steward, *Basin-Plateau Aboriginal Sociopolitical Groups*, Bulletin 120, p. 162; Julian H. Steward, "Culture Element Distributions: XXIII, Northern and Gosiute Shoshoni," *University of California Anthropological Records*, p. 264; Murphy and Murphy, "Shoshone-Bannock Subsistence and Society," p. 318; Sven Liljeblad, Letter to author, July 17, 1988; Merle W. Wells, Interview by author, Boise, Idaho, July 13, 1988.
13. Madsen, *The Lembi* pp. 25–26. Liljeblad wrote in *The Idaho Indians in Transition* that settlers from Utah "who temporarily settled on the Lemhi

River in 1855, named the native population in the valley after *Limbi*, a king in the Book of Mormon."

14. Merle W. Wells, Interview by author, Boise, Idaho, July 17, 1988. It should be noted that a Peter Weiser, or Wiser as Lewis spelled it, is the only person this river could logically be named for. The earliest maps predate the arrival of later figures, such as Jacob Weiser who was with Donald Mackenzie in 1818, or a miner of the same name who appeared at Florence during the gold rush.

15. Liljeblad, *The Idaho Indians in Transition*, p. 37. David D. Dominick, "The Sheepeaters," *Annals of Wyoming*, p. 140, states: "In Idaho the last distinct reports of a people designated as Sheepeaters came from the mountains of western Idaho between the Weiser River and the Middle Fork of the Salmon River."

16. Merle W. Wells, Interview by author, Boise, Idaho, February 24, 1986; Sven Liljeblad, Letter to author, April 28, 1988; Max G. Pavesic, *Archaeological Overview of the Middle Fork of the Salmon River Corridor, Idaho Primitive Area*, p. 4; Robert H. Ruby and John A. Brown, *Indians of the Pacific Northwest*, p. 29; Dominick, "The Sheepeaters," p. 139; Sven Liljeblad, Letter to author, April 28, 1988; Merle W. Wells, Interview by author, Boise, Idaho, June 16, 1988. Dominick, pp. 131–68, gives an in-depth review of historical studies and conclusions on the Mountain Shoshoni life-style.

17. Johnny Carrey and Cort Conley, *The Middle Fork and the Sheepeater War*, p. 156; Dominick, "The Sheepeaters," pp. 154–56; Max G. Pavesic, Interview by author, Boise, Idaho, October 21, 1985.

18. Steward, *Basin-Plateau Aboriginal Sociopolitical Groups*, pp. 38, 200. Buffalo were rare in western Idaho by the time of the arrival of white men even though fur trappers recorded an occasional sighting near the Boise area. They were extinct in the state by 1840. Murphy and Murphy, "Shoshone-Bannock Subsistence and Society," p. 319; Steward, *Basin-Plateau Aboriginal Sociopolitical Groups*, p. 165.

19. Asworth, *Hells Canyon*, p. 6; Josephy, *The Nez Perce Indians*, p. 20.

20. Madsen, *The Lemhi*, pp. 26–27; Walker, *Indians of Idaho*, p. 89; Brigham D. Madsen, *The Shoshoni Frontier and the Bear River Massacre*, p. 12.

21. Frank Harris, *The History of Washington County*, p. 56; Walker, *Indians of Idaho*, p. 91; Murphy and Murphy, "Shoshone-Bannock Subsistence and Society," p. 319.

22. Merle W. Wells, Interview by author, Boise, Idaho, March 3, 1986; Liljeblad, *The Idaho Indians in Transition*, p. 96.

23. Robert Lowie, *The Northern Shoshone, Vol. II, Part II*, p. 185.

24. Haines, *Indians of the Great Basin and Plateau*, p. 32; Steward, *Basin-Plateau Aboriginal Sociopolitical Groups*, p. 43; Max G. Pavesic, Interview by author, Boise, Idaho, October 21, 1985; Carrey and Conley, *The Middle Fork and the Sheepeater War*, p. 201.

25. Joseph Moore and Kenneth M. Ames, *Archaeological Inventory of the South Fork of the Payette, Boise County, Idaho*, p. 4; Dawn S. Statham, *Camas and the Northern Shoshoni: A Biogeographic and Socioeconomic Analysis*, pp. 65–66; Walker, *Indians of Idaho*, p. 89.

26. Washington Irving, *The Adventures of Captain Bonneville*, p. 259; Carrey and Conley, *The Middle Fork and the Sheepeater War*, p. 156; Lowie, *The Northern Shoshone*, p. 188.

27. Walker, *Indians of Idaho*, p. 101; Carrey and Conley, *The Middle Fork and the Sheepeater War*, p. 157; Lowie, *The Northern Shoshone*, p. 177.

28. Steward, *Basin-Plateau Aboriginal Sociopolitical Groups*, p. 45; Virginia Trenholm and Maurine Carley, *The Shoshonis, Sentinels of the Rockies*, pp. 15–16; Max G. Pavesic, Interview by author, Boise, Idaho, December 9, 1985; Madsen, *The Northern Shoshoni*, p. 22.

29. Sven Liljeblad, Letter to author, April 28, 1988. William C. Sturtevent, ed., *Handbook of North American Indians*, Vol. II, pp. 426–48 offers an in-depth charting of kinship terminology.

30. Asworth, *Hells Canyon*, p. 7; Robert Butler, *A Guide to Understanding Idaho Archaeology*, p. 45; Steward, *Basin-Plateau Aboriginal Sociopolitical Groups*, pp. 231, 244, 260; Liljeblad, *The Idaho Indians in Transition*, p. 12; Sven Liljeblad, Letter to author, April 28, 1988.

31. Walker, *Indians of Idaho*, p. 140; Dayley, "An Ethno-Historical Shoshone Narrative, p. 3.

32. Steward, *Basin-Plateau Aboriginal Sociopolitical Groups*, p. 247; Steward, "Culture Element Distributions," p. 279; Sven Liljeblad, Letter to author, July 17, 1988.

33. Liljeblad, *The Idaho Indians in Transition*, p. 17; Lowie, *The Northern Shoshone*, pp. 208–9.

34. Walker, *Indians of Idaho*, p. 90; Liljeblad, *The Idaho Indians in Transition*, p. 13; Madsen, *Chief Pocatello*, p. 25.

35. Walker, *Indians of Idaho*, p. 90.

36. Clark Wissler, *Indians of the United States*, p. 282; Lowie, *The Northern Shoshone*, pp. 189–90; Steward, *Basin-Plateau Aboriginal Sociopolitical Groups*, p. 201; Madsen, *The Northern Shoshoni*, p. 20; Liljeblad, *The Idaho Indians in Transition*, p. 16. Primary sources for further information on the northward spread of the horse are Francis Haines's two articles, "Where Did the Plains Indians Get Their Horses," and "The Northward Spread of Horses Among the Plains Indians," both in the *American Anthropologist*, 40 (1938).

37. Walker, *Indians of Idaho*, p. 140; Steward, *Basin-Plateau Aboriginal Sociopolitical Groups*, p. 46.

38. Liljeblad, *The Idaho Indians in Transition*, p. 16.

39. Madsen, *Chief Pocatello*, p. 26; Peterson, *Idaho*, p. 22; Sven Liljeblad, *Indian Peoples of Idaho*, p. 34; Madsen, *The Lemhi*, p. 25.

40. Steward, *Basin-Plateau Aboriginal Sociopolitical Groups*, p. 258; Alice B. Kehoe, *North American Indians, A Comprehensive Account*, p. 354; Murphy and Murphy, "Shoshone-Bannock Subsistence and Society," p. 319.

41. Harris, *The History of Washington County*, p. 32; Murphy and Murphy, "Shoshone-Bannock Subsistence and Society," p. 319.

42. Ruby and Brown, *Indians of the Pacific Northwest*, p. 29; Merle W. Wells, Interview by author, Boise, Idaho, June 16, 1988.

43. Walker, *Indians of Idaho*, p. 89; Trenholm and Carley, *The Shoshonis*, p. 25.

44. Annie Laurie Bird, *Boise, the Peace Valley*, p. 28; Merle W. Wells, Interview by author, Boise, Idaho, July 13, 1988.

45. Peterson, *Idaho*, p. 23; Liljeblad, *The Idaho Indians in Transition*, p. 19; Madsen, *The Bannock of Idaho*, p. 22; Ruby and Brown, *Indians of the Pacific Northwest*, p. 23; Max G. Pavesic, Interview by author, Boise, Idaho, December 9, 1985.

46. Liljeblad, *The Idaho Indians in Transition*, p. 16.

CHAPTER 2. THE FIRST WHITE MEN

1. Butler, *A Guide to Understanding Idaho Archaeology*, p. 45.
2. Steward, *Basin-Plateau Aboriginal Sociopolitical Groups*, p. 187. Consult journals of Lewis and Clark, August 20, 1805.
3. Consult the journals of Lewis and Clark, June 2, 1806, for details of this entry.
4. Elers Koch, "Montana, Idaho Geographic Names," *Oregon Historical Quarterly*, p. 52.
5. Ibid., p. 53.
6. Although Donald Mackenzie is credited with being the first white man to enter the Weiser country, there is no record that he made contact with the Indians in the area.
7. Nellie I. Mills, *All Along the River*, p. 15.
8. Miles Cannon, "Snake River in History," *Oregon Historical Quarterly*, p. 9; Merle W. Wells, Letter to author, July 13, 1988; Josephy, *The Nez Perce Indians*, p. 42; Rafe Gibbs, *Beckoning the Bold*, p. 12; Hiram Martin Chittenden, *History of the American Fur Trade in the Far West*, p. 195.
9. Chittenden, *History of the American Fur Trade*, p. 193.
10. Washington Irving, *Astoria*, p. 275.
11. Ibid.
12. Gordon Speck, *Northwest Explorations*, p. 304.
13. Ibid.
14. Irving, *Astoria*, p. 315.
15. Floyd Barber and Dan Martin, *Idaho in the Pacific Northwest*, p. 12; Mills, *All Along the River*, p. 14.
16. Alexander Ross, *Adventures of the First Settlers on the Oregon or Columbia River*, p. 237.
17. Cornelius Brosnan, *History of the State of Idaho*, p. 62; Peterson, *Idaho*, p. 36; Bird, *Boise*, pp. 45–48.
18. Trenholm and Carley, *Shoshonis*, p. 53.
19. Alexander Ross, *Fur Hunters of the Far West*, p. 98.
20. Josephy, *The Nez Perce Indians*, p. 50.
21. Jennie Broughton Brown, *Fort Hall on the Oregon Trail*, p. 59; Ruby and Brown, *Indians of the Pacific Northwest*, p. 44; Peterson, *Idaho*, p. 37.
22. Josephy, *The Nez Perce Indians*, pp. 50, 54.
23. Ruby and Brown, *Indians of the Pacific Northwest*, p. 44; Ross, *Fur Hunters of the Far West*, pp. 177, 190–91.
24. Ross, *Fur Hunters of the Far West*, pp. 249–55.
25. Trenholm and Carley, *The Shoshonis*, p. 54.
26. Madsen, *The Northern Shoshoni*, p. 24; Ruby and Brown, *Indians of the Pacific Northwest*, p. 44.
27. Ross, *Fur Hunters of the Far West*, pp. 252–55.
28. Josephy, *The Nez Perce Indians*, pp. 56–57.
29. Peterson, *Idaho*, p. 39.
30. Ross, *Fur Hunters of the Far West*, pp. 266–67.
31. Irving, *Astoria*, pp. 102–3.
32. Ruby and Brown, *Indians of the Pacific Northwest*, p. 52; Josephy, *The Nez Perce Indians*, p. 63. The Payette Lakes are near present-day McCall, Idaho.

33. Peter Skene Ogden, "Journal of Peter Skene Ogden; Snake Expedition, 1827–1828," *Oregon Historical Quarterly*, pp. 357–62.
34. Max Pavesic, Interview by author, Boise, Idaho, Oct. 21, 1985.
35. Ruby and Brown, *Indians of the Pacific Northwest*, pp. 53–54.
36. John Work, *The Snake Country Expedition of 1830–1831. John Work's Field Journal*, ed. Francis D. Haines, Jr., pp. 11–12.
37. "Exploration and Settlement of Salmon River," *Idaho Historical Society*, Reference Series, No. 242, November 1965.
38. Washington Irving, *The Adventures of Captain Bonneville, Vol. I*, pp. 177–78.
39. "Fur Trade Posts in Idaho," *Idaho Historical Society*, Reference Series, No. 62, October 1970.
40. Madsen, *The Lembi*, p. 12.
41. Liljeblad, *The Idaho Indians in Transition*, p. 21.
42. "Boise Shoshoni," *Idaho Historical Society*, Reference Series, No. 248, January 1979; Annie Laurie Bird, *Old Fort Boise*, p. 32.
43. Dayley, "An Ethno-Historical Shoshone Narrative," p. 3.
44. Max G. Pavesic, Interview by author, December 9, 1985.
45. Bird, *Old Fort Boise*, pp. 55–56.
46. U.S. Congress, Sen. Exec. Doc. 42, Ser. 1033, p. 137.
47. Steward, *Basin-Plateau Aboriginal Sociopolitical Groups*, p. 200.
48. Gibbs, *Beckoning the Bold*, p. 46.
49. Madsen, *Chief Pocatello*, p. 19.
50. Kehoe, *North American Indians*, p. 354; Madsen, *The Northern Shoshoni*, p. 27.
51. Ray H. Glassley, *Indian Wars of the Pacific Northwest*, p. 6; Alvin M. Josephy, Jr., *Now That the Buffalo's Gone*, pp. 74–75; Liljeblad, *Idaho Indians in Transition*, p. 30.
52. Glassley, *Indian Wars of the Pacific Northwest*, pp. 13–38.
53. Bird, *Old Fort Boise*, pp. 61–62.
54. U.S. Department of the Interior, *Annual Report of the Commissioner of Indian Affairs* (hereafter, USDI, *Annual Reports*), 1854, p. 278; Bird, *Boise*, pp. 82–24; Madsen, *The Shoshoni Frontier*, pp. 62–63; Trenholm and Carley, *The Shoshonis*, p. 186.
55. Robert R. Thompson to Joel Palmer, September 14, 1854, p. 56, U.S. Department of the Interior, Bureau of Indian Affairs (hereafter, USDI, BIA).
56. Madsen, *The Shoshoni Frontier*, p. 59.
57. Bird, *Old Fort Boise*, p. 70.
58. Nathan Olney to Palmer, July 30, 1855, I.O.R.
59. Palmer to Commissioner of Indian Affairs, March 5, 1856, I.O.R.
60. J. P. Dunn, Jr., *Massacres of the Mountains*, pp. 272–99.
61. L. U. Reavis, *The Life and Military Services of General William Selby Harney*, p. 287.
62. Trenholm and Carley, *The Shoshonis*, p. 181.
63. W. F. Lander to Commissioner of Indian Affairs, February 11, 1860, I.O.R.; U.S. Congress, Sen. Exec. Doc. 46, Ser. 1099, p. 137. Lander, the author of this executive document, gives the name "Pasheco" (Sweet Root), which is erroneous.
64. Ruby and Brown, *Indians of the Pacific Northwest*, p. 185; Trenholm and Carley, *The Shoshonis*, p. 82.
65. Madsen, *The Shoshoni Frontier*, p. 110.

66. Elwood Evans et al., *History of the Pacific Northwest*, p. 7.

67. The exact location of the attack is in some doubt. Larry Jones, Idaho State Historical Society, has completed much research on the location and his results and conclusions are noted in the "Otter Massacre Site," Idaho Historical Society, Reference Series, No. 233, March 1982.

68. Extensive coverage at the time of the incident can be located in most early newspapers. Miles Cannon, many years after the massacre, interviewed two survivors and wrote a series of articles on the details, though somewhat distorted, for the *Idaho Statesman*, July 17–August 21, 1921.

69. Walla Walla correspondent to *Portland Times*, *Oregon Argus*, Oregon City, December 22, 1860.

CHAPTER 3. MINERS AND SETTLERS

1. Jack D. Forbes, *Nevada Indians Speak*, pp. 52–81.

2. C. H. Hale to Commissioner of Indian Affairs, October 19, 1862, I.O.R.

3. USDI, *Annual Report,* 1861, p. 133 (I.O.R.).

4. Ruby and Brown, *Indians of the Pacific Northwest*, p. 239.

5. *Sacramento Daily Union*, September 16, 1861, p. 3.

6. Madsen, *The Lembi*, p. 32.

7. Defenbach, *Idaho: The Place and Its People*, p. 499; John Hailey, *History of Idaho*, pp. 33–44; Arthur A. Hart, *Basin of Gold: Life in the Boise Basin, 1862–1890*, p. 14.

8. Fred Lockley, *The Lockley Files: Voices of the Oregon Country, Vol. II*, pp. 182–83. The winter camps were near the site of present-day Cambridge, Idaho; W. W. Lloyd and Mrs. Edna A. Melhorn, "Baker County Historical Society," *Oregon Historical Quarterly*, December 1948, pp. 306–7.

9. Trenholm and Carley, *The Shoshonis*, p. 192.

10. U.S. Government Records, *The War of Rebellion: A Compilation of the Official Records of the Union and Confederate Armies*, Ser. I, Vol. L, Pt. II, pp. 42–43.

11. Ibid., p. 177.

12. Ibid., pp. 207–9.

13. Defenbach, *Idaho*, pp. 406–7.

14. U.S. Government, *War of Rebellion*, pp. 186–87; Fred B. Rodgers, *Soldiers of the Overland*, pp. 73–74.

15. Trenholm and Carley, *The Shoshonis*, p. 197.

16. Bird, *Boise, the Peace Valley*, p. 103; Hart, *Basin of Gold*, p. 14; Mills, *All Along the River*, p. 32.

17. Mills, *All Along the River*, p. 33.

18. Hailey, *History of Idaho*, pp. 50–60.

19. U.S. Government, *War of Rebellion*, p. 350.

20. Hiram T. French, *History of Idaho*, p. 37; James H. Hawley, *History of Idaho*, Vol. I, p. 688; Bird, *Boise, the Peace Valley*, pp. 168–69.

21. Hubert H. Bancroft, *The Works of Bancroft: History of Oregon, Part II, Volume XXX*, p. 495.

22. Francis Fuller Victor, "The First Oregon Cavalry," *Oregon Historical Quarterly*, June 1902, pp. 141–42.

23. Ibid.

24. Bird, *Boise, the Peace Valley*, p. 172; Victor, "The First Oregon Cavalry," p. 143.

25. Ruby and Brown, *Indians of the Pacific Northwest*, p. 194.
26. James D. Doty to Commissioner of Indian Affairs, July 6, 1863, I.O.R.
27. USDI, *Annual Report*, 1864, pp. 289–92.
28. Jerome Peltier, *Warbonnets and Epaulets*, p. 324; Liljeblad, *Idaho Indians in Transition*, pp. 28–29.
29. Hailey, *History of Idaho*, pp. 86–87.
30. *Idaho Tri-Weekly Statesman*, Boise City, Idaho Territory (hereafter I.T.), July 15, 1865, p. 2 (hereafter cited as *Idaho Statesman*).
31. Elaire Goldsmith, *In the Shadow of the Squaw*, p. 14.
32. Harris, *History of Washington County*, p. 32.
33. Goldsmith, *In the Shadow of the Squaw*, pp. 14–15; Hailey, *History of Idaho*, p. 172; Joyce Lindstrom, *Idaho's Vigilantes*, pp. 35–60.
34. Merle Wells, "Ethno History and Timber Butte Obsidian," *Idaho Archaeologist*, Fall 1980, p. 1; Sven Liljeblad, Letter to author, April 28, 1988; *Idaho Statesman*, March 13, 1869, p. 2.
35. O. O. Howard, *Famous Indian Chiefs I Have Known*, p. 259. Howard indicates Egan as half Umatilla and half Paiute, but Egan, known under several anglicized names, was Shoshoni. His Shoshoni name, Ehegande, means "The Blanket-owner." Liljeblad, Letter to author, April 28, 1988.
36. Steward, *Basin-Plateau Aboriginal Sociopolitical Groups*, p. 172; "Shoshoni and Northern Paiute Indians of Idaho," *Idaho Historical Society*, Reference Series, No. 484, November 1970; Mills, *All Along the River*, p. 48.
37. *Idaho Statesman*, March 21, 1866, p. 2.
38. Idaho Historical Society, "Bigfoot," Reference Series, No. 40, rev., November 1970.
39. USDI, *Annual Report*, 1867, p. 95.
40. Ibid., 1866, p. 38 and 1867, p. 252; Ruby and Brown, *Indians of the Pacific Northwest*, p. 195.
41. USDI, *Annual Report*, 1866, p. 38.
42. Martin F. Schmitt, *General George Crook, His Autobiography*, p. 142.
43. Ibid., p. 144.
44. Wells, "Ethno History and Timber Butte Obsidian," p. 1.
45. *Idaho Statesman*, March 28, 1867, p. 2.
46. Ibid., October 6, 1867, p. 2.
47. Ibid., October 24, 1867, p. 2.
48. Ibid., July 27, 1867, p. 2.
49. Ibid., October 5, 1867, p. 2.
50. Ibid., October 14, 1867, p. 3.
51. Idaho Historical Society, "Bigfoot," November 1970. Also, this was not a new or an isolated tactic. The Nez Perce have an old saying: "Even little Bannocks have big feet!"
52. USDI, *Annual Report*, 1867, p. 248.
53. David W. Ballard to Commissioner of Indian Affairs, September 12, 1868, USDI, *Annual Report*, 1868, p. 198.
54. USDI, *Annual Report*, 1867, p. 14; Ballard to Commissioner of Indian Affairs, August 31, 1867, USDI, BIA.
55. Madsen, *The Northern Shoshoni*, p. 54.
56. General Christopher C. Augur to President of the Indian Peace Commission, October 4, 1868, USDI, BIA.
57. USDI, *Annual Report*, 1867, p. 189.
58. *Boise Semi-Weekly Democrat*, Boise City, I.T., August 1, 1868, p. 3.

59. Charles F. Powell to Commissioner of Indian Affairs, August 15, 1868, USDI, BIA.

60. Ruby and Brown, *Indians of the Pacific Northwest*, p. 209; *Idaho Statesman*, June 16, 1868, p. 2; Schmitt, *General George Crook*, p. 159; *Owyhee Avalanche*, Silver City, I.T., July 25, 1868.

CHAPTER 4. A TIME OF TROUBLES

1. *Idaho Statesman*, August 8, 1868, p. 2.
2. Powell to Commissioner of Indian Affairs, February 3, August 28, September 7, 1868, USDI, BIA.
3. Hailey, *History of Idaho*, p. 114; "Exploration and Settlement of Salmon River," Idaho Historical Society, Reference Series, No. 242.
4. Harris, *History of Washington County*, p. 32; Grace J. Eckles, "History of Salubria Valley and Towns," in *Salute to Pioneers of Washington and Adams Counties*, ed. Elsie Marti, p. 3.
5. *Idaho Statesman*, August 25, 1868, p. 3.
6. Ibid. Located near present site of Riggins, Idaho.
7. Ibid., August 13, 1868, p. 3.
8. Ibid.
9. Ibid.
10. Ibid., September 8, 1868, p. 2.
11. Ibid., February 11, 1869, p. 2.
12. Ibid., February 9, 1869, p. 2.
13. Ibid.
14. Ibid.
15. Ballard to Powell, December 2, 1868, USDI, BIA.
16. Ibid.
17. *Idaho Statesman*, March 9, 1869, p. 3.
18. Madsen, *The Northern Shoshoni*, p. 55.
19. *Idaho Statesman*, February 11, 1869, p. 2 and March 13, 1869, p. 2.
20. Madsen, *Chief Pocatello*, p. 71; Alfred Sully to Commissioner of Indian Affairs, August 31, 1869, USDI, BIA.
21. Steward, *Basin-Plateau Aboriginal Sociopolitical Groups*, pp. 187–88; Liljeblad, *Idaho Indians in Transition*, p. 37.
22. Ruby and Brown, *Indians of the Pacific Northwest*, p. 29; *Nez Perce News*, June 9, 1881, p. 1; *Idaho Statesman*, September 12, 1878, p. 3; Steward, *Basin-Plateau Aboriginal Sociopolitical Groups*, p. 188; Floyd-Jones to Commissioner of Indian Affairs, September 28, 1869, USDI, BIA; USDI, *Annual Report*, 1869, p. 278; *Idaho Statesman*, March 13, 1869, p. 2.
23. Marti, *Salute to Pioneers*, p. 30; Hailey, *History of Idaho*, p. 140.
24. Ballard to Commissioner of Indian Affairs, April 29, 1869, USDI, BIA.
25. *Idaho Statesman*, June 5, 1869, p. 2 and July 13, 1869, p. 3; W. H. Danilson to De Lancey Floyd-Jones, July 30, 1869, USDI, BIA.
26. *Idaho Statesman*, August 14, 1869, p. 3.
27. De L. Floyd-Jones to Commissioner of Indian Affairs, August 26, 1869, USDI, BIA.
28. Ibid., September 25, 1869, I.O.R.
29. Marti, *Salute to Pioneers*, pp. 52, 91. Andy Johnson has been identified as both brother and brother-in-law of Eagle Eye in early accounts, though the latter is probably correct, and has been identified as leader of a Sheepeater

group from the South Fork of the Salmon who had a Weiser squaw (cited elsewhere). For an explanation of the Shoshonian kinship system, see Steward's *Basin-Plateau Aboriginal Sociopolitical Groups*.

30. *Idaho Statesman*, July 15, 1869, p. 3; July 27, 1869, p. 3; August 3, 1869, p. 2; November 27, 1869, p. 3; William H. Danilson to Commissioner of Indian Affairs, December 3, 1869, USDI, BIA.

31. Ruby and Brown, *Indians of the Pacific Northwest*, p. 230.

32. Secretary of the Interior to Commissioner of Indian Affairs, March 24, 27, 1871, USDI, BIA.

33. Dr. Patricia K. Ourada, Interview by author, December 10, 1985.

34. Donaldson, *Idaho of Yesterday*, p. 316.

35. *Idaho Statesman*, July 11, 1871, p. 2.

36. Donaldson, *Idaho of Yesterday*, p. 313.

37. USDI, *Annual Report*, 1870, p. 183; Johnson N. High to Commissioner of Indian Affairs, January 3, 1871, USDI, BIA.

38. Liljeblad, *The Idaho Indians in Transition*, p. 40.

39. *Idaho Statesman*, July 11, 1871, p. 2.

40. Ibid., August 29, 1871, p. 2; Montgomery P. Berry to Commissioner of Indian Affairs, September 4, 1871, USDI, BIA.

41. Ibid., September 1, 1871.

42. Marti, *Salute to Pioneers*, p. 91.

43. *Idaho Statesman*, July 11, 1872, p. 2.

44. Berry to Commissioner of Indian Affairs, January 1, 1872, May 25, 1872, USDI, BIA; Madsen, *The Northern Shoshoni*, pp. 66–67.

45. *Idaho Statesman*, July 11, 1872, p. 2.

46. Ibid., July 9, 1872, p. 2, and July 11, 1872, p. 2.

47. Madsen, *Bannock of Idaho*, p. 186; *Idaho Statesman*, August 1, 1872, p. 2.

48. Ibid., August 29, 1872, p. 2.

49. *Idaho Statesman*, July 27, 1872, p. 2.

50. Ibid., August 17, 1872, p. 3.

51. Ibid., August 29, 1872, p. 2.

CHAPTER 5. THE CLOUDS OF WAR

1. U.S. Congress, Report of the Commissioner of Indian Affairs, November 1, 1872, House Ex. Doc. 1, Ser. 1560, 42d Cong., 3d Sess., p. 453.

2. George F. Brimlow, "The Life of Sarah Winnemucca," *Oregon Historical Quarterly*, June 1952, p. 130.

3. J. W. Powell and G. W. Ingalls to Commissioner of Indian Affairs, December 18, 1973, USDI, BIA.

4. Commissioner of Indian Affairs to John P. C. Shanks, July 1, 1873, USDI, BIA.

5. Shanks, Thomas W. Bennett, and Henry W. Reed to Commissioner of Indian Affairs, November 7, 1873, USDI, *Annual Report*, 1873, pp. 157–58, 160–62.

6. Reed to Commissioner of Indian Affairs, January 12, 1873, USDI, BIA.

7. Madsen, *The Northern Shoshoni*, pp. 68–69; Dunn, *Massacres of the Mountains*, pp. 451–87; *Idaho Statesman*, April 22, 1873, p. 2.

8. Quotes are from *Idaho Statesman*, April 26, 1873, p. 2.

9. *Idaho World*, May 8, 1873, p. 2.

10. *Idaho Statesman*, May 3, 1873, p. 3.

11. Quotes are from ibid., April 23, 1873, p. 2, and May 17, 1873, p. 2.

12. Quotes are from ibid., May 15, 1873, p. 2, and September 16, 1873, p. 2.

13. Marti, *Salute to Pioneers*, p. 91.

14. Shanks, Bennett, and Reed to Commissioner of Indian Affairs, November 17, 1873, USDI, *Annual Report*, p. 158.

15. Eckles, "History of Salubria Valley and Towns," p. 6.

16. Quotes from Marti, *Salute to Pioneers*, pp. 36, 31.

17. W. V. Rinehart to Commissioner of Indian Affairs, *Annual Report*, 1878, pp. 116, 119, USDI, BIA.

18. Madsen, *The Northern Shoshoni*, p. 69.

19. Powell and Ingalls to Commissioner of Indian Affairs, December 18, 1873, USDI, *Annual Report*, 1873, p. 62; J. C. Donaldson to Commissioner of Indian Affairs, August 25, 1873, USDI, BIA; Thomas K. Cree to Commissioner of Indian Affairs, March 6, 1874, USDI, BIA; *Idaho Statesman*, June 21, 1874, p. 2; USDI, *Annual Report*, 1874, p. 54.

20. *Idaho Statesman*, October 20, 1874, p. 2.

21. Bennett to Commissioner of Indian Affairs, April 13, July 11, 1873, USDI, BIA.

22. Reed to Commissioner of Indian Affairs, September 9, 1874, USDI, *Annual Report*, pp. 284–85.

23. USDI, *Annual Report*, 1874, pp. 592–93.

24. *Idaho Statesman*, October 20, 1874, p. 2; Citizens of Weiser Valley to Bennett, September 13, 1874, Idaho Historical Society, State Archives, Territorial Records, 1874.

25. USDI, *Annual Report*, 1874, p. 76; Forbes, *Nevada Indians Speak*, p. 128.

26. USDI, *Annual Report*, 1874, p. 55; Josephy, *The Nez Perce Indians*, p. 457.

27. Madsen, *The Bannock of Idaho*, p. 196; Harrison Fuller to Commissioner of Indian Affairs, October 15, 1875, USDI, *Annual Report*, 1875, p. 311; *Idaho Statesman*, September 23, 1875, p. 2.

28. Samuel B. Parrish to Commissioner of Indian Affairs, September 2, 1875, USDI, *Annual Report*, 1875, pp. 348–49; Trenholm and Carley, *The Shoshonis*, p. 271.

29. James Wright to Commissioner of Indian Affairs, November 21, 1874, USDI, BIA.

30. James Wright to Commissioner of Indian Affairs, January 28, 30, 1875, USDI, BIA; Commissioner of Indian Affairs, 1875, USDI, *Annual Report*, p. 760.

31. Wright to Commissioner of Indian Affairs, April 12, 1875, USDI, BIA.

32. USDI, *Annual Report*, p. 760; Madsen, *The Northern Shoshoni*, p. 76.

33. *Idaho Statesman*, March 18, 1876, p. 2.

34. John Hailey to Commissioner of Indian Affairs, March 3, 1876, USDI, BIA.

35. Ibid.

36. Ray Allen Billington, *Westward Expansion*, p. 577; *Idaho Statesman*, September 7, 1876, p. 2.

37. Madsen, *The Bannock of Idaho*, pp. 199–200.

38. Rinehart to Commissioner of Indian Affairs, August 12, 1876, USDI, BIA; Ruby and Brown, *Indians of the Pacific Northwest*, p. 249; George F. Brimlow, *The Bannock War of 1878*, p. 51.

39. Brimlow, *The Bannock War*, pp. 225–26.

40. Ibid., pp. 228–29.

41. Josephy, *The Nez Perce Indians*, pp. 437–613.

42. Eugene B. Chaffee, "Nez Perce War Letters," *Idaho Historical Society, Fifteenth Biennial Report*, 1935–1936, pp. 108–9.

43. Ibid., pp. 89–90, 103–4.

44. Ibid., pp. 91–93.

45. Ibid., 106–7.

46. Ibid., pp. 95–96; Michey Aitken, *Saga of Salubria*, p. 13.

47. Chaffee, "Nez Perce War Letters," p. 109.

48. Ibid., p. 111.

49. Eckles, "History of Salubria Valley and Town," p. 6.

50. Chaffee, "Nez Perce War Letters," pp. 40, 110.

51. Ibid., p. 111.

52. Ibid., p. 123.

53. Ibid., p. 126.

54. Ibid., pp. 109, 124; Rinehart to Commissioner of Indian Affairs, August 14, 1877, USDI, *Annual Report*, 1877, p. 174.

55. Ruby and Brown, *Indians of the Pacific Northwest*, p. 249; Chaffee, "Nez Perce War Letters," p. 124.

56. Ruth B. Lyon, *The Village That Grew*, pp. 52, 54.

57. Chaffee, "Nez Perce War Letters," pp. 124–25.

58. Rinehart to Commissioner of Indian Affairs, August 14, 1877, USDI, *Annual Report*, 1877, p. 174; USDI, *Annual Report*, 1878, p. 116.

59. Ibid.

CHAPTER 6. THE BANNOCK WAR OF 1878

1. William M. Turner to Rinehart, September 10, 1877, USDI, *Annual Report*, 1878, p. 116.

2. Brimlow, *The Bannock War*, p. 47; Howard, *Famous Indian Chiefs I Have Known*, p. 269.

3. Turner to Rinehart, September 10, 1877, USDI, *Annual Report*, 1878, pp. 116–17.

4. Ibid.

5. Sarah Winnemucca Hopkins, *Life Among the Piutes: Their Wrongs and Claims*, pp. 114–43.

6. Madsen, *The Bannock of Idaho*, p. 215.

7. Forbes, *Nevada Indians Speak*, p. 133.

8. Rinehart to Commissioner of Indian Affairs, USDI, *Annual Report*, 1878, pp. 117–18.

9. Ibid.

10. Ibid.

11. Ibid.

12. Ibid., p. 119.

13. Harris, *History of Washington County*, p. 58.

14. Rinehart to Commissioner of Indian Affairs, USDI, *Annual Report*, 1878, p. 119.

15. Ibid.; *Idaho Statesman*, June 11, 1878, p. 2.
16. Rinehart to Commissioner of Indian Affairs, USDI, *Annual Report*, 1878, p. 119.
17. *Idaho Statesman*, April 30, 1878, p. 3.
18. Ibid., March 5, 1878, p. 3, and April 18, 1878, p. 2.
19. Ibid., May 9, 1878, p. 3; Donald N. Wells and Ronald H. Limbaugh, *Mason Brayman*, p. 27.
20. *Idaho Statesman*, August 1, 1878, p. 3; June 13, 1878, p. 2.
21. A. J. Barnes to Commissioner of Indian Affairs, USDI, *Annual Report*, 1878, p. 103.
22. See *Idaho Statesman*, May 25, 1878, p. 3, and Forbes, *Nevada Indians Speak*, pp. 135–38.
23. Rinehart to Commissioner of Indian Affairs, June 7, 1878, USDI, BIA; ibid., USDI, *Annual Report*, 1878, p. 119.
24. Rinehart to Commissioner of Indian Affairs, USDI, *Annual Report*, 1878, p. 119.
25. William J. McConnell, *Early History of Idaho*, p. 364.
26. General Irvin McDowell to Adjutant General, U.S. Army, June 12, 1878, USDI, BIA; *Idaho Statesman*, June 15, 1878, p. 3, June 8, 1878, p. 2, and June 11, 1878, p. 2. Several in-depth accounts exist of the Bannock War of which Brimlow's *Bannock War of 1878* is highly recommended, though the Weiser's participation is not well developed.
27. General O. O. Howard to McDowell, October 1878, U.S. Congress, House Exec. Doc. 1, Ser. 1843, 45th Cong., 3d Sess., p. 211.
28. Rinehart to Commissioner of Indian Affairs, USDI, *Annual Report*, 1878, p. 120.
29. Col. W. C. Brown, "The Sheepeater Campaign," *Idaho Historical Society, Tenth Biennial Report*, p. 25; Barnes to Commissioner of Indian Affairs, USDI, *Annual Report*, 1878, p. 103; *Idaho Statesman*, June 11, 1878, p. 2.
30. Hailey, *History of Idaho*, p. 232; Madsen, *Bannock of Idaho*, p. 217; Brimlow, *Bannock War*, pp. 91–92; *Idaho Statesman*, June 11, 1878, p. 2.
31. Brimlow, *Bannock War*, pp. 101–4.
32. *Idaho Statesman*, June 20, 1878, p. 3.
33. Howard, *Famous Chiefs I Have Known*, p. 277.
34. *Portland Morning Oregonian*, July 3, 1878, p. 1.
35. Howard to Kelton, October 1878, U.S. Congress, House Exec. Doc. 1, Ser. 1843, p. 209.
36. *Portland Morning Oregonian*, June 29, 1878, p. 1 and July 4, p. 1.
37. Howard to McDowell, October 1878, U.S. Congress, House Exec. Doc. 1, Ser. 1843, p. 211.
38. *Idaho Statesman*, June 15, 1878, pp. 2, 3 and June 29, 1878, p. 3.
39. Glassley, *Indian Wars of the Pacific Northwest*, p. 232.
40. *Idaho Statesman*, June 29, 1878, p. 1; *Portland Morning Oregonian*, June 28, 1878, p. 1.
41. Hailey, *History of Idaho*, p. 236.
42. Ibid., p. 239; *Idaho Statesman*, June 29, 1878, p. 1.
43. *Idaho Statesman*, August 31, 1878, p. 2.
44. *Portland Morning Oregonian*, July 10, 1878, p. 1; July 6, 1878, p. 1; July 9, 1878, p. 1.
45. Ibid., July 6, 1878, p. 1; July 9, 1878, p. 1.

46. Howard to Kelton, October 1878, U.S. Congress, House Exec. Doc. 1, Ser. 1843, pp. 225–27.

47. *Idaho Statesman*, July 13, 1878, pp. 2, 3.

48. Ibid., July 18, 1878, p. 3.

49. Ibid., July 11, 1878, p. 3.

50. Ibid., July 18, 1878, p. 3; July 20, 1878, p. 2.

51. J. F. Santee, "Egan of the Piutes," *Washington Historical Quarterly*, January 1985, p. 21; Brimlow, *The Bannock Indian War*, pp. 151–53.

52. There are several stories surrounding the death of Chief Egan at the hands of the Umatilla Indians. Santee's study listed in the above citation is an excellent source for further information. See *Portland Oregonian*, July 20, 1878, p. 1 and Hailey, *History of Idaho*, p. 242.

53. Captain Miles to Howard, and Col. Frank Wheaton to McDowell, July 19, 1878, U.S. Congress, House Exec. Doc. 1, Ser. 1843, pp. 226, 177–78.

54. *Idaho Statesman*, August 31, 1878, p. 3.

55. See Wheaton to Major John Green, July 18, 1878, U.S. Congress, House Exec. Doc. 1, Ser. 1843, p. 177; quote is from same document, Howard to Kelton, July 19, 1878.

56. See ibid., Howard to McDowell, October 1878, p. 226 and Howard to Kelton, July 19, 1878, p. 177.

57. Ibid., p. 178; Cornoyer to Commissioner of Indian Affairs, July 19, 1878, USDI, BIA.

58. Howard to Kelton, July 19, 1878, U.S. Congress, House Exec. Doc. 1, Ser. 1843, p. 178.

59. *Portland Morning Oregonian*, August 3, 1878, p. 1.

60. *Idaho Statesman*, July 20, 1878, p. 2 and July 30, 1878, p. 3.

61. Howard to McDowell, October 1878, U.S. Congress, House Exec. Doc. 1, Ser. 1843, p. 229.

62. *Idaho Statesman*, August 10, 1878, p. 2; August 15, 1878, p. 3; *Portland Morning Oregonian*, August 3, 1878, p. 1.; Brimlow, *The Bannock Indian War*, pp. 159–60.

63. *Idaho Statesman*, August 1, 1878, p. 3.

64. Sven Liljeblad, Letter to author, April 28, 1988; Merle W. Wells, Interview by author, Boise, Idaho, June 16, 1988.

65. Hailey, *History of Idaho*, p. 245.

66. Howard to Kelton, August 12, 1878, U.S. Congress, House Exec. Doc. 1, Ser. 1843, pp. 185–86.

67. *Portland Morning Oregonian*, August 2, 1878, p. 2.

68. *Idaho Statesman*, August 6, 1878, p. 2.

69. Ibid., August 10, 1878, p. 3.

70. Lyon, *Valley of Plenty*, p. 97; *The Village That Grew*, pp. 55–56.

71. Major A. H. Nickerson to McDowell, August 6, 1878, U.S. Congress, House Exec. Doc. 1, Ser. 1843, p. 184; *Idaho Statesman*, July 20, 1878, p. 2; August 8, 1878, p. 3.

72. Madsen, *Bannock of Idaho*, pp. 223–25; Howard to McDowell, September 13, 1878, U.S. Congress, House Exec. Doc. 1, Ser. 1843, p. 192.

73. *Idaho Statesman*, August 21, 1878, p. 3.

74. Ibid., August 27, 1878, p. 3.

75. *Nez Perce News*, Lewiston, June 9, 1881, p. 1.

76. *Idaho Statesman*, August 29, 1878, p. 3.

77. Howard to Kelton, August 29, 1878, U.S. Congress, House Exec. Doc. 1, Ser. 1843, p. 189.

78. *Idaho Statesman*, August 31, 1878, p. 3; Hopkins, *Life Among the Piutes*, pp. 197–98, 260.

79. *Idaho Statesman*, September 7, 1878, p. 3; September 12, 1878, p. 3.

80. Ibid., September 21, 1878, p. 3 and October 1, 1878, p. 2.

81. Ibid., September 14, 1878, p. 3, September 26, 1878, p. 3, and October 17, 1878, p. 2. This was probably Indian Charley's little group, who were later found in the area. Literature of the time indicates that Eagle Eye and his family were then still located in the Seven Devils Mountains.

82. Madsen, *Bannock of Idaho*, p. 227.

83. Madsen, *The Northern Shoshoni*, pp. 85–86.

84. W. V. Rinehart, "War in the Great Northwest," *Washington Historical Quarterly*, April 1931, p. 97.

CHAPTER 7. A FINAL RESISTANCE

1. *Idaho Statesman*, October 22, 1878, p. 3.

2. Brimlow, *The Bannock Indian War*, p. 177.

3. *Idaho Statesman*, March 22, 1879, p. 4.

4. George E. Shoup, *History of Lemhi County*, p. 28.

5. Aaron F. Parker, "Forgotten Tragedies of an Indian War," *Sheepeater Indian Campaign*, p. 12.

6. Carrey and Conley, *The Middle Fork and the Sheepeater War*, p. 179.

7. Peterson, *Idaho*, pp. 85–86.

8. Carrey and Conley, *The Middle Fork and the Sheepeater War*, p. 160.

9. Kelton to Howard, May 1, 1879, U.S. Congress, House Exec. Doc. 1, Ser. 1903, pp. 155–56.

10. Ibid.

11. Several good sources exist for a more detailed study of the Sheepeater Campaign. Carrey and Conley's *The Middle Fork and the Sheepeater War*, and the *Sheepeater Indian Campaign*, published by the Idaho County Free Press, are well researched.

12. McConnell, *Early History of Idaho*, p. 365.

13. Howard to Kelton, September 1879, U.S. Congress, House Exec. Doc. 1, Ser. 1903, p. 157.

14. *Idaho Statesman*, July 8, 1879, p. 3.

15. Howard to Kelton, September 1879, pp. 157–58.

16. Ibid.

17. Ibid.

18. Brown, "The Sheepeater Campaign," p. 14.

19. Howard to Kelton, September 1879, U.S. Congress, House Exec. Doc. 1, Ser. 1903, p. 159. Lt. Catley was later court-martialed for his timid actions against the Indians.

20. Bernard to Howard, August 19, 1879, U.S. Congress, House Exec. Doc. 1, Ser. 1903, p. 161.

21. Carrey and Conley, *The Middle Fork and the Sheepeater War*, pp. 190–91.

22. Howard to Kelton, September 1879, U.S. Congress, House Exec. Doc. 1, Ser. 1903, p. 161.

23. Ibid., p. 159.

24. Ibid., p. 160.
25. *Idaho Statesman*, September 25, 1879, p. 3.
26. Brown, "The Sheepeater Campaign," pp. 23–27.
27. Ibid.
28. Ibid.
29. Howard to Kelton, October 9, 1879, U.S. Congress, House Exec. Doc. 1, Ser. 1903, p. 163; Hopkins, *Life Among the Piutes*, pp. 241–42, 244.
30. Liljeblad, *Idaho Indians in Transition*, p. 39.
31. Parker, "Forgotten Tragedies of an Indian War," p. 17; *Idaho Statesman*, September 20, 1879, p. 2; September 23, 1879, p. 3.
32. Brown, "The Sheepeater Campaign," p. 27.
33. *Idaho Statesman*, June 22, 1880, p. 3.
34. Ibid.
35. Rinehart to Commissioner of Indian Affairs, USDI, *Annual Report*, 1880, p. 142; Howard to Kelton, September 18, 1880, U.S. Congress, House Exec. Doc. 1, Ser. 1952, p. 189.
36. Howard to Kelton, September 18, 1880, U.S. Congress, House Exec. Doc. 1, Ser. 1952, p. 189.
37. *Nez Perce News*, June 9, 1881, p. 1; *Idaho Statesman*, August 14, 1880, p. 3; October 12, 1880, p. 3; Howard to Kelton, September 18, 1880, U.S. Congress, House Exec. Doc. 1, Ser. 1952, p. 190.
38. *Idaho Statesman*, October 5, 1880, p. 3.
39. Ibid., May 28, 1881, p. 3.
40. Ibid., June 4, 1881, p. 3; *Nez Perce News*, June 9, 1881, p. 1.
41. Wheaton to Howard, 1882, U.S. Congress, House Exec. Doc. 1, Ser. 2010, p. 148.
42. The Malheur Reservation was returned to public domain by executive order on May 13, 1883. (Report of the Commissioner of Indian Affairs, October 10, 1883, U.S. Congress, House Exec. Doc. 1, Ser. 2191, p. 55.)
43. Indian Charley, a Nez Perce member of the Weiser group, should not be confused with Eagle Eye, who is a Shoshoni and an entirely separate individual, though it is thought they were related through marriage. *Idaho Statesman*, April 5, 1898, p. 6.
44. Liljeblad, *Idaho Indians in Transition*, p. 40.
45. Gratia Bacon Matthews, *Round Valley, My Home in Covered Wagon Days*, p. 49.
46. Report of the Commissioner of Indian Affairs, October 10, 1883, p. 55, USDA, BIA.
47. Madsen, *The Lembi*, p. 116; Diffendaffer, *Council Valley*, p. 187.
48. Marti, *Salute to Pioneers*, p. 12.
49. Cort Conley, Letter to author, December 13, 1986.
50. The relationship between Andy Johnson the Sheepeater and Andy Johnston the ditch rider at Notus, Idaho, is unknown. It is thought that the Indian was an employee of the Johnston Brothers of lower Boise prior to the Indian wars. The origin of his white name is lost in antiquity.
51. Lyon, *The Village That Grew*, p. 45; Mills, *All Along the River*, p. 228.
52. Mills, *All Along the River*, p. 228.
53. Liljeblad, *The Idaho Indians in Transition*, p. 40.
54. Dayley, "An Ethno-Historical Shoshone Narrative," p. 5.
55. *Idaho Statesman*, April 5, 1898, p. 6.
56. Dayley, "An Ethno-Historical Shoshone Narrative," p. 5.

57. *Idaho Statesman*, January 26, 1888, p. 3.

58. Ibid. Also, the families of J. W. Cook, a miner, and those of Joe L. Reed and William Parrish, owners of two early-day sawmills there, became quite close friends with Eagle Eye's family. Ella Parrish, whose sister was Maggie Knox (Knox and Parrish were partners at the Soldier Creek Mill), were extremely close and their children spent the summers playing with those of the Indians, creating a bond that lasted for more than seven decades between the families. Mills, *All Along the River*, p. 228.

59. Report of the Commissioner of Indian Affairs, USDI, *Annual Report*, 1890, pp. 76–78, and USDI, *Annual Report*, 1893, p. 135.

60. E. M. Yearian to Commissioner of Indian Affairs, August 23, 1899 (I.O.R.)

61. Donaldson, *Idaho of Yesterday*, p. 333.

62. Abraham L. Rinearson, Survey Report, May 1892, Idaho State Historical Society, Water Resources File.

63. Howard to Asst. Adjutant General, September 18, 1880, U.S. Congress, House Exec. Doc. 1, Ser. 1952, Vol. 1, p. 189; *Emmett Index*, April 14, 1894, p. 4; *Idaho Statesman*, April 5, 1898, p. 6.

64. Report of the Commissioner of Indian Affairs, USDI, *Annual Report*, 1895, p. 22.

65. Ibid., p. 23.

66. Ibid., USDI, *Annual Report*, 1896, pp. 28–29.

67. *Emmett Index*, May 30, 1896, p. 1.

68. Wells, "Ethno History and Timber Butte Obsidian," p. 1.

69. *Emmett Index*, June 6, 1896, p. 4.

70. Wells, "Ethno History and Timber Butte Obsidian," p. 3.

71. *Emmett Index*, June 25, 1897, p. 1; *Idaho Statesman*, April 5, 1898, p. 6.

72. Sven Liljeblad, Letter to author, April 28, 1988.

73. *Idaho Statesman*, April 5, 1898, p. 6.

74. R. S. Browne to Shoup, January 31, 1898, USDI, BIA.

75. *Idaho Statesman*, April 5, 1898, p. 6.

76. C. A. Warner to Commissioner of Indian Affairs, June 27, 1898, USDI, BIA; Madsen, *The Northern Shoshoni*, p. 138.

77. USDI, *Annual Report*, 1898, p. 66, and USDI, *Annual Report*, 1899, p. 564 (I.O.R.).

78. Kehoe, *North American Indians*, p. 355.

79. Liljeblad, *Idaho Indians in Transition*, p. 40.

80. Ibid.

81. Ibid.

82. Yearian to Commissioner of Indian Affairs, August 23, 1899, USDI, BIA.

83. Ibid., USDI, *Annual Report*, 1898, p. 146.

84. Crowder, *Tendoy, Chief of the Lembis*, p. 77.

85. Sven Liljeblad, Letter to author, April 28, 1988. In addition, John High-Eagle, also spelled John (High) Eagle, was for many years a respected figure of the Weiser group at Fort Hall, as was an elderly Charles Eagle, described by Liljeblad to the author as either a brother or cousin to John. Any speculation that Charles may have been Young Charley, and the half-Nez Perce son of Indian Charley, is unfounded.

86. Liljeblad, *Idaho Indians in Transition*, p. 40.

87. Wells, "Ethno History and Timber Butte Obsidian," p. 3.

88. Mills, *All Along the River*, p. 226.

CHAPTER 8. CONCLUSION.

1. Madsen, *The Northern Shoshoni*, p. 230.
2. Wells, "Ethno History and Timber Butte Obsidian," pp. 1–3.
3. Dayley, "An Ethno-Historical Shoshone Narrative, pp. 3–13.

BIBLIOGRAPHY

Aitken, Mickey. *Saga of Salubria*. Weiser, Idaho: Signal American Printers, 1951.

Ames, Kenneth M. *Archaeological Investigations in the Payette River Drainage, Southwestern Idaho 1979–1981*. Boise, Idaho: Boise State University, 1981.

Ashworth, William. *Hells Canyon, The Deepest Gorge on Earth*. New York: Hawthorn Books, Inc., 1977.

Bailey, R. G. *River of No Return*. Lewiston, Idaho: Lewiston Printing, 1983.

Bancroft, Hubert H. *The Works of Bancroft: History of Oregon, Part II, Volume XXX*. San Francisco: The History Company, Publishers, 1888.

Barber, Floyd R., and Martin, Dan W. *Idaho in the Pacific Northwest*. Caldwell, Idaho: Caxton Printers, Ltd., 1961.

Billington, Ray Allen. *Westward Expansion*. New York: Macmillan Publishing Co., Inc., 1974.

Bird, Annie Laurie. *Boise, the Peace Valley*. Caldwell, Idaho: Caxton Printers, Ltd., 1934.

———. *Old Fort Boise*. Parma, Idaho: Old Fort Boise Historical Society, 1971.

Boise Semi-Weekly Democrat. Boise, Idaho: August 1, 1868.

Brimlow, George F. *The Bannock Indian War of 1878*. Caldwell, Idaho: Caxton Printers, Ltd., 1938.

———. "The Life of Sarah Winnemucca," *Oregon Historical Quarterly*, June, 1952.

Brosnan, Cornelius J. *History of the State of Idaho*. New York: Charles Scribner's Sons, 1918.

Brown, Jennie Broughton. *Fort Hall on the Oregon Trail*. Caldwell, Idaho: Caxton Printers, Ltd., 1932.

Brown, Col. W. C. "The Sheepeater Campaign," *Idaho State Historical Society, Tenth Biennial Report*, 1926.

Butler, Robert. *A Guide to Understanding Idaho Archeology*. 2d rev. ed. Pocatello, Idaho: Idaho State University Museum, 1968.

Cannon, Miles. "Snake River in History," *Oregon Historical Quarterly*, March-December, 1919.

Carrey, Johnny, and Cort Conley. *The Middle Fork and the Sheepeater War*. Cambridge, Idaho: Backeddy Books, 1977.

Chaffee, Eugene B. "Nez Perce War Letters," *Idaho State Historical Society, Fifteenth Biennial Report*, 1936.

Chittenden, Hiram Martin. *History of the American Fur Trade in the Far West*. Vol. 1. Stanford: Academic Reprints, 1954.

Conley, Cort. Letter to author, December 13, 1986.

Crowder, David L. *Tendoy, Chief of the Lembis*. Caldwell, Idaho: Caxton Printers, Ltd., 1969.

Dayley, Jon P. "An Ethno-Historical Shoshone Narrative, Pie Nimmin Naakkanna, 'How We Lived Long Ago.'" *Idaho Archaeologist*. Spring, 1986: 3–13.

Defenbach, Byron. *Idaho, the Place and Its People, Vol. I*. Chicago: The American Historical Society, 1933.

Diffendaffer, Marguerite L. *Council Valley: Here They Labored*. Council, Idaho: Worthwhile Club of Council, 1977.

Dominick, David D. "The Sheepeaters." *Annals of Wyoming*, vol. 36. Cheyenne, Wyo.: Wyoming State Archives and Historical Department, 1964.

Donaldson, Thomas. *Idaho of Yesterday*. Caldwell, Idaho: Caxton Printers, Ltd., 1941.

Dunn, J. P., Jr. *Massacres of the Mountains*. New York: Capricorn Books, 1886.

Eckles, Grace J. "History of Salubria Valley and Towns." In Elsie Marti, *Salute to Pioneers of Washington and Adams Counties*. Council, Idaho: Council Printing and Publishing, 1984.

Emmett Index. Emmett, Idaho: April 14, 1894; May 30, 1896; June 6, 1896; June 25, 1897.

Evans, Elwood, et al. *History of the Pacific Northwest, Vol. II*. Portland, Oreg.: North Pacific History Co., 1889.

Forbes, Jack D. *Nevada Indians Speak*. Reno: University of Nevada Press, 1969.

French, Hiram T. *History of Idaho*. New York: Lewis Publishing Co., 1914.

Gibbs, Rafe. *Beckoning the Bold*. Portland, Oreg.: Durham and Downey, Inc., 1976.

Glassley, Ray H. *Indian Wars of the Pacific Northwest*. Portland, Oreg.: Binfords and Mort, Publishers, 1953.

Goldsmith, Elaire. *In the Shadow of the Squaw*. Caldwell, Idaho: Caxton Printers, Ltd., 1953.

Gulick, Bill. *Chief Joseph Country*. Caldwell, Idaho: Caxton Printers, Ltd., 1981.

Hailey, John. *History of Idaho*. Boise, Idaho: Syms-York Company, Inc., 1910.

Haines, Francis. *Indians of the Great Basin and Plateau*. New York: G. P. Putnam and Sons, 1970.

________. "Where Did the Plains Indians Get Their Horses?" *American Anthropologist*, 40. 1938.

________. "The Northward Spread of Horses Among the Plains Indians." *American Anthropologist*, 40. 1938.

Handbook of North American Indians, ed. William C. Sturtevent, Washington, D.C.: Smithsonian Institution, 1986.

Hanley, Mike. *Owyhee Trails*. Caldwell, Idaho: The Caxton Printers, Ltd., 1973.

Harris, Frank. *History of Washington County*. N.p.

Harris, Jack. "The White Knife Shoshoni of Nevada." *Acculturation in Seven American Indian Tribes*. Ralph Linton, ed. New York: Appleton Company, 1940.

Hart, Arthur A. *Basin of Gold: Life in the Boise Basin, 1862–1890*. Boise, Idaho: Lithocraft, Inc., 1986.

Hart, Newell. *The Bear River Massacre*. Preston, Idaho: Cache Valley Newsletter Publishing Co., 1982.

Hawley, James H. *History of Idaho*. 4 vols. Chicago: S. J. Clark Publishing Company, 1920.

Hopkins, Sarah Winnemucca. *Life Among the Piutes: Their Wrongs and Claims*. Boston: Cupples, Upham, & Co., 1883.

Howard, Helen A., and McGrath, Dan L. *War Chief Joseph*. Lincoln: University of Nebraska Press, 1941.

Howard, O. O. *Famous Indian Chiefs I Have Known*. New York: The Century Publishing Company, 1908.

Idaho Historical Society. Water Resources File. Survey Report, Abraham L. Rinearson, May 3, 1892.

———. Idaho Territorial Records. 1874. Petition from the Citizens of the Weiser Valley.

———. "Bigfoot," Reference Series, No. 40, November 1970 rev.

———. "Boise Shoshoni," Reference Series, No. 248, January 1979.

———. "Exploration and Settlement of Salmon River," Reference Series, No. 242, November 1965.

———. "Fur Trade Posts in Idaho," Reference Series, No. 62, October 1979.

———. "Otter Massacre Site," Reference Series, No. 233, March 1982.

———. "Shoshoni and Northern Paiute Indians of Idaho," Reference Series, No. 484, November 1970.

Idaho Tri-Weekly Statesman (Idaho Statesman). Boise, Idaho: 1865–1921.

Idaho World. Idaho City, Idaho: May 8, 1873.

Irving, Washington. *The Adventures of Captain Bonneville*. 2 vols. "Pawnee Edition." New York: C. P. Putnam's Sons, 1898.

———. *Astoria*. Portland, Oreg.: Binfords and Mort, Publishers, 1967.

Josephy, Alvin M., Jr. *The Nez Perce Indians and the Opening of the Northwest*. Lincoln: University of Nebraska Press, 1965.

———. *Now That the Buffalo's Gone*. Norman: University of Oklahoma Press, 1984.

Kehoe, Alice B. *North American Indians: A Comprehensive Account*. New Jersey: Prentice-Hall, Inc., 1981.

Koch, Elers. "Montana, Idaho Geographic Names," *Oregon Historical Quarterly*, March, 1948.

Langford, Nathaniel P. *Vigilante Days and Ways*. New York: A. L. Burk Co., 1890.

Lewis, Meriwether, and William Clark. *Original Journals of the Lewis and Clark Expedition*. 8 Vols. R. G. Thwaites, ed. New York: Dodd and Mead, 1904–05.

Liljeblad, Sven. *Indian Peoples of Idaho*. Pocatello: Idaho State University Library, 1957.

———. *The Idaho Indians in Transition, 1895–1860*. Pocatello: Idaho State University Museum, 1972.

———. Letters to author. April 28, 1988; July 17, 1988.

Lindstrom, Joyce. *Idaho's Vigilantes*. Moscow: University Press of Idaho, 1984.

Lloyd, W. W. and Melhorn, Edna A. "Baker County Historical Society," *Oregon Historical Quarterly*, December, 1948.

Lockley, Fred. *The Lockley Files: Voices of the Oregon Country. Vol. II*. Eugene, Oreg.: Rainy Day Press, 1981.

Lowie, Robert H. *The Northern Shoshone. Vol. II, Part II*. New York: Museum of Natural History, 1909.

Lyon, Ruth B. *The Village That Grew*. Boise, Idaho: Lithocraft, Inc., 1979.

———. *Valley of Plenty*. Boise, Idaho: Capitol Lithograph and Printing, 1968.

McConnell, William J. *Early History of Idaho*. Caldwell, Idaho: Caxton Printers, Ltd., 1913.

Madsen, Brigham D. *The Bannock of Idaho*. Caldwell, Idaho: Caxton Printers, Ltd., 1958.

________. *Chief Pocatello, "The White Plume"*. Salt Lake City: University of Utah Press, 1986.

________. *The Lemhi: Sacajawea's People*. Caldwell, Idaho: Caxton Printers, Ltd., 1979.

________. *The Northern Shoshoni*. Caldwell, Idaho: Caxton Printers, Ltd., 1980.

________. *The Shoshoni Frontier and the Bear River Massacre*. Salt Lake City: University of Utah Press, 1985.

Marti, Elsi. *Salute to Pioneers of Washington and Adams Counties*. Council, Idaho: Council Printing and Publishing, 1984.

Matthews, Gratia Bacon. *Round Valley, My Home in Covered Wagon Days*. N.p. 1981.

Mills, Nellie I. *All Along the River*. Montreal: Payette Radio Limited, 1963.

Moore, Joseph, and Kenneth M. Ames. *Archaeological Inventory of the South Fork of the Payette River, Boise County, Idaho*. Boise, Idaho: Boise State University, 1979.

Morning Oregonian. Portland, Oreg.: Various dates in 1878.

Murphy, Robert F., and Yolanda Murphy. "Shoshone-Bannock Subsistence and Society." *University of California Anthropological Records*, 16:7. Berkeley: University of California Press, 1960.

Newell, Helen M. *Idaho's Place in the Sun*. Boise, Idaho: Syms-York Company, 1975.

Nez Perce News. Lewiston, Idaho: June 9, 1881.

Ogden, Peter Skene. "Journal of Peter Skene Ogden: Snake Expedition, 1827–1828." *Oregon Historical Quarterly*. Portland, Oreg.: 1911.

Oregon Argus. Oregon City, Oreg.: December 22, 1860; July 27, 1863.

Ourada, Patricia K., ed. *Indian Peoples of Idaho*. Boise, Idaho: Boise State University Press, 1975.

________. *The Indian in United States History*. Boise, Idaho: Boise State University Press, 1979.

________. Interview by author. December 10, 1985.

Owyhee Avalanche. Silver City, Idaho: July 25, 1868.

Parker, Aaron F. "Forgotten Tragedies of an Indian War." *The Sheepeater Campaign*. Grangeville, Idaho: Idaho County Free Press, 1968.

Pavesic, Max G. *Archaeological Overview of the Middle Fork of the Salmon River Corridor, Idaho Primitive Area*. Boise, Idaho: Boise State University, 1978.

________. Interviews by author. September 23, 1985; October 14, 1985; October 21, 1985; November 19, 1985; December 9, 1985.

Peltier, Jerome. *Warbonnets and Epaulets*. Montreal: Payette Radio Limited. N.d.

Peterson, F. Ross. *Idaho: A Bicentennial History*. American Association for State and Local History; New York: W. W. Norton and Company, Inc., 1976.

Reavis, L. U. *The Life and Military Services of General William Selby Harney*. St. Louis: Bryan, Brand & Co., 1878.

Rees, John E. *Idaho Chronology, Nomenclature, Bibliography*. Chicago: W. B. Conkey Company, 1918.

Rinehart, W. V. "War in the Great Northwest," *Washington Historical Quarterly*, April, 1931.

Rodgers, Fred B. *Soldiers of the Overland*. San Francisco: The Grabhorn Press, 1939.

Ross, Alexander. *Adventures of the First Settlers on the Oregon or Columbia River*. London: 1949.

________. *Fur Hunters of the Far West*. Norman: University of Oklahoma Press, 1956.

Ruby, Robert H., and Brown, John A. *Indians of the Pacific Northwest*. Norman: University of Oklahoma Press, 1981.

Sacramento Daily Union. Sacramento, Calif.: September 16, 1861.

Santee, J. F. "Egan of the Piutes," *Washington Historical Quarterly*, January, 1935.

Schmitt, Martin F. *General George Crook, His Autobiography*. Norman: University of Oklahoma Press, 1960.

Shoup, George E. *History of Lemhi County*. Boise, Idaho: Idaho State Library, 1969.

Speck, Gordon. *Northwest Explorations*. Portland, Oreg.: Binfords and Mort, Publishers, 1954.

Statham, Dawn S. *Camas and the Northern Shoshoni: A Biogeographic and Socioeconomic Analysis*. Boise, Idaho: Boise State University, 1982.

Steward, Julian H. *Basin-Plateau Aboriginal Sociopolitical Groups*. Washington, D.C.: Smithsonian Institution, Bureau of American Ethnology, 1938.

________. "Culture Element Distributions, XXIII: Northern and Gosiute Shoshoni." *University of California Anthropological Records*, 8:3. Berkeley: University of California Press, 1960.

Steward, Julian H., and Erminie Wheeler-Voegelin. *Paiute Indians III: The Northern Paiute Indians*. New York: Garland Publishing, Inc., 1974.

Stewart, Omer. *Indians of the Great Basin*. Bloomington: Indiana University Press, 1982.

Swanton, John R. *The Indian Tribes of North America. Bulletin 145*. Bureau of American Ethnology. Washington, D.C.: Government Printing Office, 1952.

Talkington, H. L. *Heros and Heroic Deeds of the Pacific Northwest, Vol. I*. Caldwell, Idaho: Caxton Printers, Ltd., 1929.

Trenholm, Virginia, and Maurine Carley. *The Shoshonis: Sentinels of the Rockies*. Norman: University of Oklahoma Press, 1964.

U.S. Congress. House Executive Document 1, serial no. 1560, 42d Cong., 3d sess.

________. House Executive Document 1, serial no. 1843, 45th Cong., 3d sess.

________. House Executive Document 1, serial no. 1903, 46th Cong., 2d sess.

________. House Executive Document 1, serial no. 1952, 46th Cong., 3d sess.

________. House Executive Document 1, serial no. 2010, 47th Cong., 1st sess.

________. House Executive Document 1, serial no. 2191, 48th Cong., 1st sess.

U.S. Congress. Senate Executive Document 42, serial no. 1033, 36th Cong., 1st sess.

________. Senate Executive Document 46, serial no. 1099, 36th Cong., 2d sess.

U.S. Department of Interior. Bureau of Indian Affairs. Record Group 75. *Records, documents, and incoming correspondence from Idaho, Washington, Oregon, Nevada, Utah, and Montana agencies and superintendencies (1824–1881)*. Washington, D.C.: Indian Office Records.

________. *Annual Reports of the Commissioner of Indian Affairs*. 1854–1899.

U.S. Department of War. Executive Division. Adjutant General's Office, Old Files. General O. O. Howard, Annual Report, 1878, (Inclosure). Map: *Plan of Operations of the Department of the Columbia, 1878*.

U.S. Government Records. *The War of Rebellion; a Compilation of the Official Records of the Union and Confederate Armies*. Series I, Vol. L, Part II. Washington, D.C., 1897.

Victor, Francis Fuller. "The First Oregon Cavalry," *Oregon Historical Quarterly*. June, 1902.

Walker, Deward E., Jr. *Indians of Idaho*. Moscow: The University Press of Idaho, 1982.

Wells, Donald N., and Limbaugh, Ronald H. *Mason Brayman*. Boise, Idaho: N.p., n.d.

Wells, Merle W. "Ethno History and Timber Butte Obsidian." *Idaho Archaeologist*. Fall 1980: 1–3.

________. "The Sheepeaters." John Carrey and Cort Conley. *The Middle Fork and the Sheepeater War*. Riggins, Idaho: Backeddy Books, 1977.

________. Interviews with author. February 24, 1986; March 3, 1986; April 21, 1986; June 16, 1986; October 22, 1986; June 16, 1988; July 13, 1988; July 17, 1988.

Wissler, Clark. *Indians of the United States*. New York: Doubleday and Co., Inc., 1940.

Woodman, George. *Mining Map of Oregon and Idaho, 1864*. Berkeley: The Bancroft Library, University of California.

Work, John. *The Snake County Expedition of 1830–1831. John Work's Field Journal*. Francis D. Haines, Jr., ed. Norman: University of Oklahoma Press, 1971.

INDEX